Born to E[ntertain]

DeLois LaDelle
A Life Story

"Born to Entertain!" by DeLois LaDelle. ISBN 978-1-62137-033-8 (softcover).

Published 2012 by Virtualbookworm.com Publishing Inc., P.O. Box 9949, College Station, TX 77842, US. ©2012, DeLois LaDelle. All rights reserved. No part of this publication may be reproduced, stored in a retrieval system, or transmitted in any form or by any means, electronic, mechanical, recording or otherwise, without the prior written permission of DeLois LaDelle.

Manufactured in the United States of America.

- My Childhood

- On MY Own

- Showbusiness

- Family Matters

- Mrs. Jack LaDelle

Addendem: Lovin' to Entertain
My Life in Pictures

A NOTE OF THANKS

I would like to thank my brother Ronald for always being there when I need him and having dinner with me every Tuesday night.

I would also like to thank Diana Spencer for all of her help with my pictures, ads, and writeups, and her placement of those in my book. She has been such a big help through all of the writing, thank again!

And a special thanks to my brother Bob, my "adopted" son, Blaine; friends, students, my hairdresser, Sandy Burns who keeps my hair looking great, my dog and the Lord for letting me have the good things in life that I have had!

I hope you enjoy the book!

Delois

My Childhood

My mother, Bonnie Jean Neely was only 17 years old when she married my father, John Phillips. My mother helped my father run a small restaurant in a little town of Sprigg, West Virginia. When my mother found out she was pregnant she went to stay with my dad's mother so she wouldn't be alone while my father worked.

I was born March 15th, 1937 in a house on the hill with the help of my father's mother, a neighbor, and a country veterinarian. I weighed five pounds and eight ounces. I had reddish brown hair and brown eyes. My mother was very proud of me and gave me the name of Delois and my father gave me my middle name of Jean after my mother.

Sprigg, West Virginia was a little town with a bar, grocery store, post office and a gas station. Most of the homes were on a hill. The famous Hatfield and McCoy family was across the way from us.

My mother was so excited that three months after I was born she bundled me up in my uncle's truck and drove me to meet my grandfather, Clarence Neely, in Tomahawk, Kentucky. He was a tall lean man with a dark complexion, who always somehow reminded of Abraham Lincoln. He lived in a "holler" in a large home in the middle of a huge farm, with miles and miles of beautiful green valleys and giant hills, with cows, chickens, pigs, "out houses" and everything else you can imagine on a farm.

For those of you that are not familiar with a "holler" you generally drive down a road in the middle of trees and hills and a person meets you at the front of the road with a rifle asking you "Where are you going?" If you are family or friends of one of the many families who live back in the hills they will let you in, if not you will not be able to go back and if you try they will shoot!

My granddaddy was so happy to see us when my mother ran inside of the old wooden house and laid the small bundle in his lap that he held me in his arms for many hours. When I was a baby my mother and I spent much of our time going from Sprigg to Tomahawk.

I don't remember much about my young childhood except making mud pies with the next door kids; cleaning the bowls out that mom made our dessert in; wearing mom's high heels; eating those big thick chocolate pies that grandma made and playing with my little black cocker spaniel I owned with four white paws and huge brown eyes, Yes, all of these things I look back on as my childhood with fun and laughing, dancing, and playing.

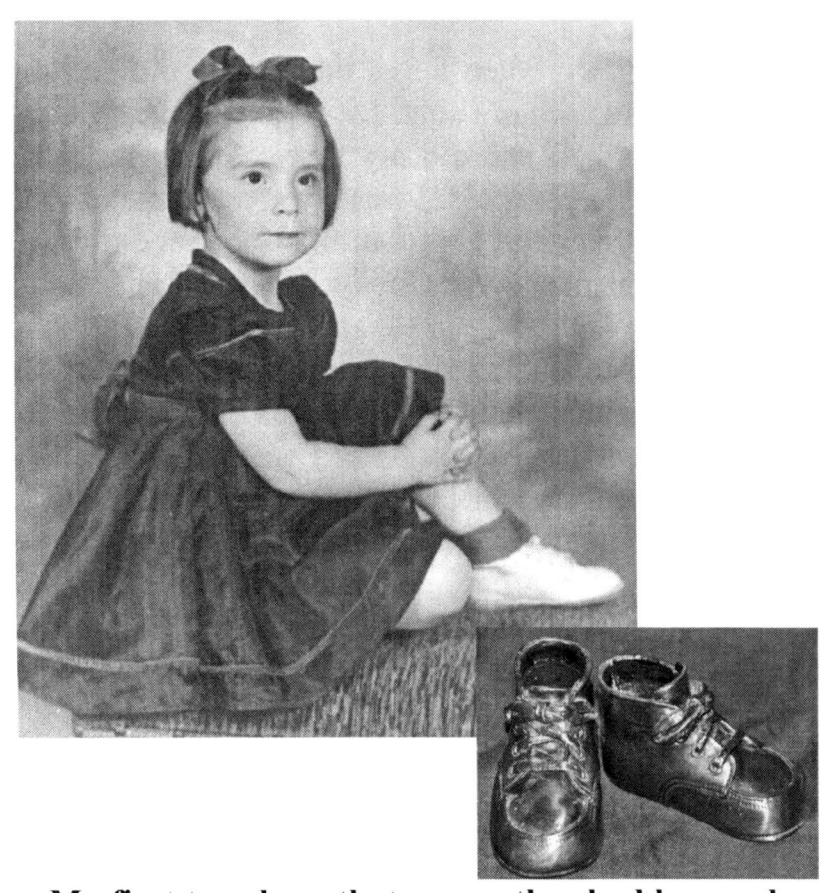

My first tap shoes that my mother had bronzed.

❧ Born to Dance

My mother and father separated when I was three years old and my mother and I moved to Akron, Ohio to live with my aunt. I was given dancing lessons when I was three and a half and did my first solo in Muriel Kelleher's dance review at 4 ½ years old. I was given the name of "Miss Personality" on the program and kept that title for years afterwards. I won first prize in a talent show at Goodyear Theater at 5.

My mother then remarried a man by the name of Mr. King. I don't remember much about him, she was only married to him for a very short time. After that was over I was alone or with a babysitter for much of the time while my mother worked hard to support me. She worked in many different places and it often felt very lonesome. I was pretty much my own boss and became somewhat spoiled. The rest of my early childhood was mostly happy. I remember going back and sitting on my grandfather Neely's knees and listening to old stories of many years ago and about the legends of the south.

❧ School Days

It was at the age of six that I started ballet and it was the first time that I had ever danced in a class and I found it nice to play and dance with new friends. I remember trying to imitate my teacher and try to dance just like her for I thought she was the best dancer in the world.

We moved from place to place until I started fifth grade. Then finally settled down and I began to go to Howe Grade School. At first I was very shy and kept to myself.

Then, because of a small, white haired English teacher, I began to do things that I had never done before. I'll always remember Ms. Dora Harper. She had sparkling blue eyes that danced when she became excited. She became interested in me because of the stories I wrote. Most of them were imaginative and many were humorous. I had two main characters that I called Herkamer and Jerkemer, which I carried through most of my stories. These characters became well known through school, Miss Harper would have me read them to all her classes and then some of the teachers hearing about the stories, would have me come to their classes and read them. I became so interested in this new adventure that I began making puppets and using odd names for them, this started them on the road to popularity. I was called up to do skits for paper sales with my puppets; and many days I was let out of class to give

4

puppet shows to the children in other classes. I also danced in the talent shows and was at one time, chosen Queen of Howe School and was given a silver crown. This was a big thrill for me.

Then one summer at the beginning of the eighth grade, I changed my activities in school. I was going to my grandmother's house and started across the street when a car which was racing over the hill, hit me throwing me several feet, leaving my body in a limp pile at the edge of the street and I was rushed to the hospital.

TWO PEDESTRIANS were among those suffering minor injuries. They were Mrs. Mary A. Lachok, 43, of 957 Brown st., and Delois Phillips, 14, of 596 W. Bowery st.

Mrs. Lachok was struck by a car at S. Broadway and E. Center st. The driver, David Gibson, 54, of 848 N. Firestone blvd., was cited for failing to yield the right of way to a pedestrian. The Phillips girl was hit at W. Bowery and Bartges sts.

While Mario DelPozzo, 29, of 1190 Dayton st., was turning a corner slowly at Dayton st. and Iuka av., his two-year-old daughter, Diana, fell from the car. She was treated for minor injuries.

Others treated at hospitals for minor injuries were Richard P. Kelly, 60, of 695 Weber av.; Gilbert Landwehr, 39, of Tallmadge, and Eva L. Edwards, 74, of 403 Rexford st.

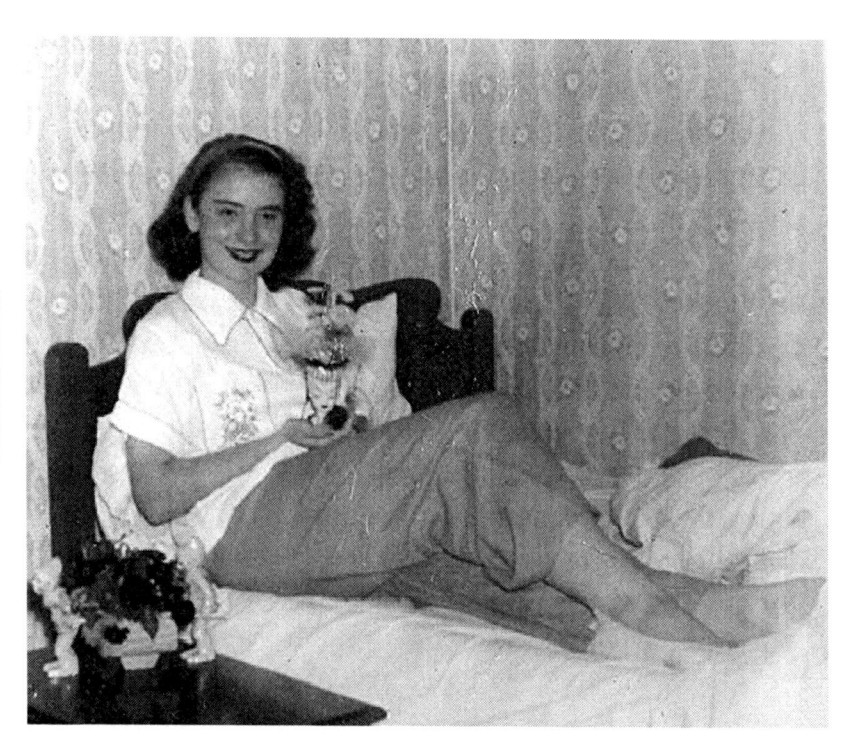

The doctor could not believe that there were no bones broken and that I came out of it with only a broken thumb, badly bruised legs and a huge lump on my head. I was sent home and was told to stay in bed for several weeks. I remember worrying about my dancing and having the fear of maybe not being able to walk again, During the next few weeks I received cards, flowers and so many of my friends visited, even Mrs. Harper and my dance teacher Muriel Kelleher. I was given strict orders from my doctor that I was not allowed to dance for several months, but when I was alone I would try to get my feet and legs to move again, just like I wanted them to. Then came the day that I was finally allowed to return to school and was also given the approval to dance again. I was very happy and excited.

✥ Summer Vacation

It was the following summer that we spent our vacation visiting my grandfather Clarence Neely in Kentucky. My Aunt Evie and Uncle Buck lived there with him. In the hills they had breakfast (usually pancakes, eggs, bacon or sausage, and fried potatoes home made butter, jelly, and gravy and biscuits), dinner (meat, cornbread, potatoes, gravy, vegetables, and pie), supper (left overs from dinner and usually a few added dishes). Granddad would get up at 5:00 in the morning go out and milk the cows and feed the chickens and the livestock and pigs and then he would come back in for breakfast. I used to go out with my granddad and he always had to watch me. One of my favorite times was playing in the hay loft at the top of the barn and riding the horses. I remember an episode with the big, black bull. My grandfather had warned my cousin and I to stay away from the bull when we had red on, but the two of us decided to play a little game with the bull and I got my red sweater and stood in the middle of an old log bridge which was only wide enough for one person at a time and waved the sweater at the bull knowing that he wouldn't be able to cross the bridge. The bull puffed and snorted and got mad at me and pawed the ground until my grandfather came and stopped us. I would tie the cows tails together, ride the donkey so I could get "paw paws (a fruit that tastes like sweet bananas) off the tree. I always loved visiting granddad. I don't know how he put up with me but he was always good and always loved me.

I remember being very afraid of snakes and I used to dream of them. I told my granddad that one night and he said that probably was because when I was a very little baby I was sitting in the grass in front of the house and he was on the front porch watching me when a great big rattle snake rose up almost right next to me, he grabbed his shot gun and shot it before it could harm me. He said I probably kept the memory in my head even though I was a baby when it happened. I have to admit I still hate snakes to this day.

Shortly after that we went to Sprigg and I would play with other kids in the street. We played outside a bar and could hear all the music. My granddaddy Hiram Phillips taught me to sing and the first song I ever sang was one they played on the jukebox in the bar called "They say that God Don't Make Honky-tonk Angels" I can't believe I can still remember the lyrics: "As I sit here tonight the jukebox playing a song bout the wild side of life too many times married me still think they're single and cheats on a true and trusted wife." "They say that God don't make honky-tonk angels" as it says in the words of this song, too many times married men still think they're single and have caused many a good girl to go wrong."

Moving Along

At the end of the seventh grade my mother remarried; he was a tall, good-looking blond haired air force man. He was good to me when I was a kid, but as time went on, he was not good to my mother. The marriage did not last very long. But during it while I was in eighth grade in school, my mother gave birth to a little blond haired, blue eyed baby brother, he was named Ronald Thomas Hargraves.

I was very happy to have a little brother. I even remember having to learn to change diapers, feeding and playing with him. Not long after he was born my mother received a divorce. We moved upstairs over a hardware store. I would stand on top of a box so I could reach the stove and my mother taught me to cook. Everything was from scratch. One of the first things I made was baked beans. I would have dinner ready for mom when she came home from work. I practically raised my brother because my mother had to work to support us.

I never cared too much about boys as many of my girlfriends did in grade school. I kept up with my dancing and worked hard on my grades until I met a boy by the name of Allan Morgan who threw stones at my window and waived at me while my mom was at work. He was a big bully and always protected me when I left school. I thought he could do no wrong. Most of the kids thought he was so tough but I can remember asking him to baby sit my brother Ron while Mom took me to do a show and he said he would if I didn't tell anyone at school! He was always very sweet to me.

7

The next year I began to attend South High School. My first day I went to register at school and with that came the lipstick tubes, elevator tickets, and all the other things used to tempt and tease us young, wide eyed freshman. I remember all my teachers: Miss Botzum, taught English, very strict and very stern, Miss Kendall, my Algebra teacher who always seemed to be a little late, my drama teacher Mr. Noble Elderkin who I thought was the greatest person living. He taught me to do pantomimes and I remember doing several pantomimes at the Weathervane Playhouse for him. He was always very outspoken and said whatever came to his mind.

My freshman year was very happy because I was teaching dancing for Muriel Kelleher, my dance teacher.

Not long after that I went to Cleveland and appeared on the Giant Tiger Amateur Hour with Gene Carrol and won first prize, a fifty dollar war bond for my dance. I also came in second at a talent show held at South High. It was at this time that I also started my professional dancing.

8

By the time I reached the tenth grade I had won first prizes on the Opportunity Hour with Jack Clifton, and Audition Ambition.

```
                            LEROY-YALE
                            WEWS - Thurs. Mar. 27, 1952
                            TV OPPORTUNITY HOUR - 11 PM

        VIDEO                       AUDIO
                            JACK: Once again it's prize winner
                            time. Time for us to present the
                            second prize winning amateur act of
                            last Thursday night's Opportunity Hour
                            competition. And here she is Miss
                            DeLois Phillips with her pantomimic
                            impression of Betty Hutton singing
                            "A Square in the Social Circle".
FAST DISSOLVE TO            SECOND PRIZE WINNER...DeLois Phillips...
PRIZE WINNER ON             Pantomime..."A Square in the Social
SET 1, SUPER BALOP          Circle"
SECOND PRIZE WINNER


DISSOLVE TO JACK            APPLAUSE
ON SET 1, ENTER
PRIZE WINNER

CLOSE-UP OF WATCH           PRESENTS PRIZE

                            JACK: And now let's meet Act 9 on
                            tonight's parade of amateur talent.
ACT 9 ENTERS to             BRIEF INTERVIEW AND CUE INTO ACT
SET 1


FAST DISSOLVE TO            ACT 9...Joan Carollo...Tap Dance...
ACT 9, ON SET 2,            "Git Happy"
SUPER BALOP
CONTESTANT #9


FADE TO BLACK               APPLAUSE
BRIEFLY, THEN BRING
UP CLIFTON ON SET 2
WITH ACT 10
```

Plus it was during that time that I met a man by the name of Kenny Monroe and was doing many shows with the old vaudevillian. Kenny was a funny guy and a good entertainer. He was sure that I was going to become a famous entertainer. He said I had a lot of talent and he asked my mother if I could do shows with him around town. She said yes and as a result I worked places like the Elks, Moose club and anywhere else Kenny wanted me to go. I loved entertaining.

> CELEBRATE THE FOURTH AT THE
> **WHITE HOUSE INN**
> MONROE and PHILLIPS
> Terrific Show for the Holidays
> TWO SHOWS NIGHTLY—10:30 - 1:00
> ELEANOR and Her Orchestra
> SAME POLICY—No Cover or Minimum Charge
> Warren's Favorite PUBLIC Night Spot

He taught me a lot about show business, how to always look at your audience and to always do as good a show as possible because people came to see you and you should try to never disappoint them! Even if you were sick and didn't feel well, the show must go on!

I started to dance with Jim Hovis at the first of my tenth grade, we also started dating and he asked me to the Masked Ball at the Armory. I was thrilled. We even got our picture taken and put in the paper. We were thrilled to be in the Sunday paper on the front page of the second section of the Review Journal. He was a sweet guy; and we kept in touch for quite a while.

Then at the end of the tenth grade my mother remarried a man named William W. Evans.

LOIS PHILLIPS AND JIM HOVIS
Crossing the floor between dances.

He already had three children who lived with him. Carol, the oldest with blond hair and blue eyes, Willie blue eyes and brown hair, and a son named Binx who was 14 and had brown eyes and hair with freckles sprinkled across his nose and looked enough like me to be my real brother. We moved at the end of the year in a large home on Jefferson Avenue in Akron. It was then that I learned I would have to transfer to Buchtel High School the next year. I couldn't imagine leaving South High and all my close friends but at least I got to finish out the year with them.

My brother Ronnie and I were always very close because I always took care of him when Mom worked. I thought Bill was very tough on him and he was always very tough with me too. I think at first we were both unhappy. Bill wanted to adopt us but I said no, I wanted to keep my name but Mom made the decision that he could adopt Ron. I thought Bill was so cruel sometimes, he would take Ron out to the shed and spank him and I would cry. My little brother was so important to me; it would really hurt me when he would correct him for anything.

That summer I worked very hard and saved my money for the first two months of the summer because I wanted to go to New York City for a dancing convention with my teacher. My new stepfather Bill decided Ron and I should work every summer. My first job was at Woolworths and although I liked it my dad decided that driving me there every morning before he went to work was hard for him so he decided I should work in his office. I started working that next summer in my dad's office. I thought it would be a "piece of cake" because he was my father, but he was harder on me than anyone else in the office and I learned to type, answer the phone make copies and any other thing he could think of for me to do. I would come home from school and ask him a question and he would say look at the wall full of books, you look it up and if you don't understand it I will help you. I thought he was so mean when I was little but later on in my life I realized that he taught me more than anyone in my life. He was my stepfather but the only father I really had in my life.

New York City

Just two weeks before time to go to New York I received a letter from Mr. Markert, the head of the Rockettes telling me I could audition when I arrived in New York, My mother explained that she had wrote him and asked him if I would be able to audition when I was there. I was very excited and for the next two weeks, I think I walked on air. Then my dance teacher and I received our reservations for the Hotel Taft in New York and our airline tickets.

At last the morning came for us to leave and I was thrilled when we arrived at the Akron airport and saw the big plane we were to ride on and just a bit frightened. Soon we were on the plane waving out the window to my family. The hostess told us to tighten our seat belts and we were on our way. We were served lunch and about two hours later we reached the airport and from the air I saw the Statue of Liberty.

Now, as we rode into town I could see the tall skyscrapers as our cab took us to the hotel. We went up to the room and unpacked and went to sign up for the dance convention. We started our lessons from a teacher for the convention by the name of Jack Stanley.

After I finished I went down the hall and watched a teacher by the name of Ernest Carlos. He was teaching down the hall from us and I was stunned by Carlos and his dancing. He was a tall man with sleek black hair and when he tap danced it looked like his feet never left the floor, yet you could hear every tap as clear as a bell. I asked what he charged and there was no way I could afford it so I just stood there and tried to learn it. The next day after our regular lessons I found my way to Carlos again and he looked up at me and said for me to "come on in, honey; you have fancy feet!" I told him I couldn't afford the lessons and he asked me how long I would be there and I told him just a week so he told me I had good feet and to come on in. He was wonderful to me and told me some day he was sure I would be a star. I learned five routines while I was there and notes for some more.

I also attended lessons from a Jack Stanly who was teaching for the convention. My schedule started at when I woke up at seven in the morning grabbed coffee and rolls in the room and went to Carlos class at eight and worked till ten, then went with Muriel to Jack Stanley's lesson and worked till 12:00, ate lunch at 12:30 went back to Carlos at 1:00 till three, then went back to the room, got a shower and got dressed and went sight seeing until six. Went back to the room and changed and went to dinner at seven and went to see a Broadway musical or some place we wanted to see. We visited the Statue of Liberty, Central Park, Radio City Music Hall, Chinatown and the Empire State building. We saw Fifth Avenue and walked down it and bought a bracelet at Tiffany's. We dined at Taffinetti's The Brass Rail, and went to the Copacabana to see a show with the dancing teachers.

I can dance it — I can prance it
I can tap it gay and sprightly
I can swing it — Buck 'n Wing it
Or just sort of sand it lightly

I can shuffle it a little bit
or really make it hep
But no matter how I do it
You can bet I'm right in step

to wish you
A MERRY CHRISTMAS AND A HAPPY NEW YEAR

Ernest Carlos

Then came the day I was to audition for the Rockettes. I was very frightened when I walked in the Radio City Music Hall. I was taken upstairs to a fabulous rehearsal hall and a dressing room. I changed and went out and was introduced to Mr. Russell Markert. He was a tall man with a black handle bar mustache. I did a straight tap and then he asked me to show him some of my kick work. I did several different kinds of kicks and he was very pleased. I laughed when he told me that he would let me perform in the Rockettes but that I had to just smile and dance and not put all the actions in it that I did. Rockettes are supposed to all look and act alike. That part I knew would be hard for me because I was such a "ham" He told me if I could stay I could start rehearsing that next day or I could come back in two weeks and could start for the rest of the summer with the Rockettes. I was on cloud nine and hugged Muriel and told her the news when I walked out of the studio. I called my mother and asked if I could stay because Muriel could stay for another week with me.

For the next two days I rehearsed for the show and started the third day. I loved it and we had rehearsal as well. Radio City had rooms upstairs.

Then one night Muriel couldn't go to dinner with me and she told me if I was going to dinner not to go to far from the hotel. So I walked down the street and saw a sign that said Monsigners, a French restaurant. It was beautiful, violin players and a very nice atmosphere. I had so much fun I sat at a table and looked at the menu, there were no prices on it so I thought wow it must really be cheap. The waiter came over and welcomed me and took my order. The violin players came over and asked what song I would like to hear, I told them and they played it……the second song I sang with them, needless to say I had so much fun and everyone was so nice. When my bill came I was horrified, I didn't have that kind of money with me, I only had five dollars, I told the waiter and he said he would have to talk to the maître d.' The maître d' came over and talked to me and asked me if I was going to meet someone and when I told him no he said they had made a mistake on my check and asked me how much I had with me. When I told him he told me that my bill was $3.00. I thanked him so much and I gave $1.00 to the violin players. Everyone applauded when I left and I hugged them all! I went back to the hotel and told Muriel my experience.

Many years later she told me about the very expensive and nice restaurant and she was surprised I was treated so well. The next morning I got up and went to rehearsal.

Everything went very well until I was almost through with my two months that I could stay. One morning I had decided to show Mr. Markert how good my fan kick was. His was wonderful and I practiced every day to get mine as big as his, so when I did it for him I pulled a ligament and I cried because I knew I was finished dancing until it healed. Mr. Markert tried to comfort me and told that he would call me next summer and invite me again. I cried as I limped back to my hotel and I got a plane home the next day.

But as I flew home I was so thankful to do all the things a I did and meet all the people I met and I could hardly wait to tell my friends and family.

Showplace

RADIO CITY MUSIC HALL

My first week home was fun because I was reliving my trip to New York. When they asked about my trip, I was more than happy to tell them every detail! The second week found me very bored with the everyday procedure of home and I missed the excitement of the "big city" and interesting people I met. The next week I spent getting ready to attend a new school with kids I didn't know. Willie, my sister tried to ease my tensions by telling me that she would go with me to sign up and try to introduce me to her friends and as many of the juniors that she knew My first two weeks of Buchtel I found most of my teachers were nice to get along with and very helpful; the kids however, were somewhat different. Upon my arrival I learned a new word called "clicks." Many of these kids would say Hi to me but that was as far as it went. After the first month of Buchtel I wanted terribly to go back to South High where all the kids were all just in one group and nobody was treated differently than anyone else. I came home many nights crying but soon faced the fact that I had to be a big girl and realize that I should take the bad with the good.

I began teaching dancing more nights for Muriel and I started appearing regularly on a WAKR-TV show called the Teen Who Club. I worked with a tall dark haired girl by the name of Carol Ann Zaldie; a short red-haired girl called Connie Burelson; and a tall nice looking guy by the name of Jack Bennet. The three of them did pantomimes and I was the featured dancer although I also started doing pantomimes as well later.

Gene Davis was an Akron disc jockey who was the master of ceremonies on the show. We all had a lot of fun doing the show and we all jokingly called Gene "Pops" and acted as one big happy family. We had stars on the show from time to time and one time we had Florin Ziebach on the show and I danced while he played the violin. I always got so excited when we met performers on the show.

At then end of my junior year I helped my sister, Willie, and did the chorography for class night. This became very hard for me because I not only had to do my television shows but I had to teach dancing at the studio and to the kids at school besides getting my schoolwork and taking exams. I got to know the kids better through teaching them and found out that most of them were pretty swell after you got to know them. The school year ended and I found myself with no money to go to New York. I wrote a letter to Mr. Markert telling him the situation and asking him to forgive me for letting him know so late. He wrote back telling me that it was alright and not to worry because since I was going back to school in September I could only work for three months anyway and if I decided against attending college I could always write him and he would use me then. I did quite a bit of professional work that summer but saved very little of it and instead spent it on clothes and new costumes.

The start of my senior year found me very busy. I was going to school, coming home going down to the studio and working till 8:30 coming home, doing my homework and going to bed around 11:00 every other night. Monday and Friday nights I did my television shows and Sunday we had rehearsal for it and on Saturdays after teaching till 4:30 I did shows in clubs with Kenny Monroe. The only nights I had home with nothing to do was Wednesdays. My folks decided to put their foot down and declared I was doing too much for a girl my age so I had to quite my television show but I did not give up my teaching dancing. I learned a lot about television and producing a show and I loved entertaining I would have liked to stay. I didn't quit till the 3rd of January and for the rest of the month I didn't know what to do with myself. Then my older sister Carol asked me to help her and her sorority sisters with a number they wanted to do so they could win. I accepted her plea and taught the girls routines and they did it in April and won the first place trophy. I was very proud of them. Not long after that I was asked by Mr. Kidder, the music teacher at Buchtel to teach a group of kids a dance for the May Festival. I started teaching them and not long after that some guys from Akron U who belonged to the Phi Delta Theta Fraternity asked me to teach them a skit and help them produce their act. So I decided that since they were very good singers they could sing "Davy Crocket" and act it out with singing and dancing. They were pleased with the idea and began to work with it.

It was just before this that my mother brought a new addition to our family making it three girls and three boys. He was nine pounds and eight ounces and was called Robert Lee. It was almost four weeks after the baby's arrival on March 14th that I started teaching the May Festival routine and about two weeks before the may Festival at school that I stared working with the Deltas. Two days after the May Festival the Phi Deltas had their Casaba and they won the first place trophy, which was the first time that they had even placed in five years. I was very proud. Then the next week I started teaching Can Can to twenty senior girls for class day.

It was now close to my getting my diploma and I spoke with my dad and asked him if I could go on the road as an entertainer. We talked for quiet some time, he told me he really wanted me to be a school teacher but if I had my heart set on being an entertainer he would let me do it if I went one year to college. He said show business is so insecure, one day you might be down at the bottom and then the very next day you might be sitting on top of the world with your name in lights to prove it. Then again you might go for many years, just barely getting by and leading an unhappy and poor life. He also said it can be a heart breaking business that you could work for years and never reach the top. It not only depends on a boss, like many other jobs but also depends on billions of people as well. We finally made a deal that I would go one year to college and at the end if I still wanted to go into show business he would let me. So I decided to go one year to Kent State University.

On My Own
From Studies to Stage

My time at Kent State was fun and busy. I made new boyfriends, performed shows on weekends and kept teaching dancing for Muriel. I auditioned for a play and got the part in it. It was my first time in that kind of a production and I really enjoyed it. I was in every show at Kent and really studied hard but I also had a good time!

At the end of the year I still wanted to go on the road. I told my dad that I would keep learning things on the road and I would make him proud of me. He told me that he would keep his word if that was what I really wanted to do. I had been corresponding with an agent down in Florida by the name of Roland Muse and he started booking me at places on the way to Florida. I decided to use the name Lois instead of DeLois when I first started on the road because I had always had so many problems with DeLois through school and everyday life with people calling me Delores, Delvis, Delowise, and numerous other weird pronunciations. Looking back through the years and seeing a lot of my old write-ups with people like Stan Kenton, Charlie Spivak, Johnny Desmond, Jerry Lester, Henny Youngman, Jerry Van Dyke, Claude Thornhill, Wayne King, all of them are with just Lois Phillips. My agent made me have pictures taken in costumes to promote my shows. He would send them to places to get me work.

CHIPPEWA LAKE PARK NEWS

Big Timers At Free Shows

Sunday brings one of the top attractions to the stage of the Chippewa lakefront theater, when the 35-piece Rubber City Concert Band, directed by Mark Houser, opens at 6:30 with an hour and a half of band music. This concert will be given under the sponsorship of the Woman's Club of Chippewa on the Lake, and the American Federation of Musicians performance fund.

Sunday, August 24, the concert and show will feature the prize-winning barbershop quartets of northern Ohio, and a choir of 50 voices. Don't miss this!

Last Sunday one of the finest stage shows ever presented at Chipp, playing to 3000 spectators, found the Kenny Monroe band on stage behind the balancing act of Don and June King, Lois Philips, and Carol Parker.

Stan Kenton

Lois Phillips and Jerry Van Dyke, both appearing at Gus Stevens, pause here to say "cheeze" for our Coast Wiz cameraman

On the Road

My first place I played was Winona, Minnesota. When I arrived at the hotel I decided to go to the library while I was there and do a little research on Winona. I found out that it was named after Princess Wenonah who was the daughter of Wapasha, the chief of tribe that had a village name Keoya. Wenonah, her name means the first born daughter. Wenonah was so beautiful that she was often called the 'wild rose of the prairie." I wanted to empress my dad that I was still learning even though I was in show business. When I was on my own I began to appreciate all the things my stepfather taught me. Back in those days most of the places I was booked were supper clubs. I was doing primarily a tap dance act. I did 25 minutes of tap dancing.

My agent told me he wanted me to work Florida so he could get a lot of people in to see me because I was so new to the business. He booked me in many clubs on the way to Florida. He said he was going to book me in a strip club and the comic and I would work between the strippers. That was a whole new experience in my life. On the way down to Florida one of the other shows he booked me on was in Tampa. Everyone on the show was a star (from the old days including Vaughn Monroe) except me and a monkey act. But out of all the stars on the show Vaughn was the only one that came over and complimented me and told me some day I would be a headliner, that I had a lot of talent. I was speechless. It was just one day and the next day I was on my way to Florida.

The strip club was a real experience, I was so naive when I went on the road, I really didn't know what a stripper was and when I saw them come out (in those days) in a beautiful gown and walk around the stage I thought they were going to dance any minute but all they did was take off their clothes so to me they were pretty boring. Then because all of the girls solicited drinks the owner decided I should too. In those days I didn't drink so he sat me next to a big planter and told me when the guy wasn't looking just to throw my drink in the planter. I wasn't very good at that and about the third guy who bought me a drink excused himself and I immediately pored the drink in the planter but he was just picking something up that he dropped on the other side of me and it landed on his head instead of the planter. Well the owner decided I was not good enough to do that so he just had me dance when one of the strippers were busy which was fine with me although some nights the comic and I were the only people most of the guys saw when they came him in. He told me that night that I was a good performer but not right for a strip club, but he was sure he would see me perform at other places one day.

Then one night Charlie Spivak came in and told me that my agent asked him to stop by and see me work because he needed an opening act for his show at the Langford Hotel in Winter Park, Florida. Charlie and I talked for some time and he hired me that night. I opened with Charlie at the Langford Hotel that next week. Charlie had a wonderful band and I really enjoyed working with him. Then one day at rehearsal he took me to the side and said that I had such a great body that the agents might try to talk me into being a stripper and he thought I should start singing.

TOWN HOUSE SUPPER CLUB
TOP Entertainment and Dancing Nitely
The *Langford* Hotel
Winter Park

I had always sang little funny songs before I started my dancing but not really sang. Charlie was so good to me, he taught me how to breath (like a horn player) so I could really hold notes for a long time. He gave me a list of songs to learn, and some of them were slow and I told him I didn't think I could do slow songs because I felt better if I could move a lot because I thought I could sell it better but he told me that I would be able to sing those slow songs if I practiced. So one night after I finished my act he said to the audience, how would you like to hear Lois sing? They all applauded and I was scared to death. I walked out on the stage and sang Frank Sinatra's My Way. The audience was wonderful. So after I changed from my costume Charlie made me put on a gown and stand with the band and sing the rest of the night with them. I had so much fun; it was great to be the girl singer with the band!!

Charlie started writing arrangements (called charts in those days) for all the songs I sang and the dance numbers. Charlie didn't work all the time in those days, but because I had to work, he booked me with lots of the "old timers" like Claude Thornhill, whom I thought so much of; then I started singing in my act. It was at that point that I became a dancer and singer. Then Charlie got me a job with Wayne King. We started in Chicago and then got on a bus and did "one nighters!" That was a whole new experience for me. The guys in the band were fun to travel with although I had to sit up front across from Wayne. If we were running late going somewhere many times I had to change into my gown in the back of the bus, the guys in the band were my curtain!!

Wayne taught me a lot. He would make me sing a song when someone requested it even if I didn't know it. He would give me the music, make me go off to the side of the stand and go through it and then come out and sing it. He said people would appreciate it even if I didn't do it perfect because it was their song. I found out he was right!! Then when our last night in Chicago was coming up I sent my mom and dad tickets to come to Chicago and watch the show. I knew my dad would really enjoy it because Wayne was one of his favorite bands. After working with Wayne my dad was thrilled that I was an entertainer because he got to see me work with one of his favorite band leaders!!! At last he thought I was a star! I received the sweetest letter from him when he got home.

✥ Southward

From there I started working my way through the south. I worked Baton Rouge, Louisiana; Memphis, Tennessee; Black Poodle Lounge in Nashville, Tennessee; Iroquois Supper club in Louisville, Kentucky.

ISSUE OF OCTOBER 23, 1957

ISSUE OF NOVEMBER 6, 1957

December, 1959

LOIS PHILLIPS, lovely exotic who plays leading clubs in Miami Beach, also playing return engagement;

26

I became a headliner and was making really great money. I worked in a place called Pine Hurst, North Carolina at Pine Hurst Country Club. It was a very nice club and I had a wonderful time. It was there that one of the maîtred's told me a table of people wanted me to join them for a drink. I went over to the table and they sat me next to a very handsome guy and we started talking. In those days my first question to new people was "what do you do?" and when I asked him that the whole table started laughing. He smiled and told me he was the usher at the local theater, they all started laughing again. I found out later he was a famous golfer by the name of Julius Boris. My father was so upset when I told him I didn't know what Julius Boris did!!!! I had a lot of fun with him and he asked me out to play golf quite often and then one day he asked me to come out dressed up because some newspaper people were going to be there and of course I went to the golf course the next day and newspaper people were there and took a picture of me in my dress and high heels with golf clubs in my hands! Everybody got a big kick out of that!!!

Jack LaDelle

In this country, I worked places like Shelby, Montana; Port Huron, Flint, and Detroit, Michigan; Biloxi, Mississippi; Great Falls, Montana; Gahanna, Cincinnati, Akron, and Cleveland, Ohio; Indianapolis; Baton Rouge, Louisiana; Saint Petersburg, Tampa, Fort Lauderdale, Miami, Orlando, Stuart, and Boca Raton, Florida; Indian, Birmingham, Alabama; Nashville, Memphis, Tennessee; Atlanta, Georgia; New York City, New York; Dallas, Texas; Charleston, West Virginia; Bismarck, North Dakota; South Dakota; Washington, DC; Idaho; Erie, Pennsylvania; Chicago, Illinois; Missouri; Arkansas; Denver, Colorado; Pine Hurst, North Carolina. And I'm sure a few more I missed!

I was working all over the United States then I was booked in Portland, Oregon. I headlined in a club there and packed the place. The owner decided I was doing such a good business that he held me over another week even though he had another headliner coming in. When I looked out and saw the marquee the next day it said Lois Phillips and Jack LaDelle.

I had never heard of him but I thought that it would be a new experience to work with a headliner. In those days they almost always had a line of girls that opened the show and they told me that Jack was really something and almost all of them had gone out with him. When he came in for rehearsal with the band that afternoon I had just finished rehearsing a new number that I was going to add when I heard him talking loudly to the owner that he was the headliner and he was not going to share the marquee with anyone. That was when I thought what a "full of himself" guy he was so I just went up to the owner in front of him and told him that he could put my name anywhere, I would still have the people and I could work anywhere on the show and I would still impress the audience! And I walked away…. That was my first introduction to him.

As the week went on he tried to become friends and asked to take me out; I thought he was a good entertainer, but I didn't care much for him. The next week I received a call from my agent telling me he changed the place where I was going to next to Spokane, Washington. I told him I didn't care. Well, I packed up and arrived in Spokane and when I got to the club Jack was there too. I found out he was working there as well. I didn't know that he was friends with my agent and had asked him to book me with him. But I had already decided I still didn't want anything to do with him. We worked together the first two weeks and on that Sat. I was invited to a friend's party. When I arrived, all of the people there had dates except me and Jack. And Jack was tending bar. I spent most of the evening talking with Jack. He was very interesting. We started dating after that. I found myself falling in love with him.

I was surprised. The more we were together the more I didn't want to leave him, even though at that time my career started to look brighter. I wanted to marry Jack. But he said he just wasn't ready for that yet. So I decided to book myself with an agent out of New York. I was from the "old school" and I thought if he doesn't love me enough to want to spend the rest of his life with me then I needed to move on. And I did!

When I worked in Montana I had so many surprises. The scenery was beautiful and the mountains fantastic. The first night I drove there the snow was really deep. When I stood in it, it reached my bottom so when I got into the motel I called to see if they were going to be open that night for me to work there. The owner said, "Come on in, honey this is just a little snow "squall" So I did go in and the place was loaded!! I loved the people and the places I worked in Great Falls, Montana. I had the most fun in Billings, Montana.

The place that I worked was run by a guy that the Mafia had shipped out of Las Vegas. He cooked and also was the owner. He was a funny little Italian guy but was very sweet to me. He wore his chef's uniform every night as he always cooked in the kitchen and when I did my show he would come out of the kitchen and sit in the front row!! I got a big kick out of him. He made fabulous Italian food. He always had a Sunday buffet and sometimes would have a stuffed pig. His food was wonderful and I always really enjoyed it. He always kidded me and told me I ate like a bird, a vulture!!! He picked up my option and I was there almost two months. I had to leave after that because my agent had me booked in Vegas. In those days Jack was working at the top of the Dunes when Ralph Morgan's orchestra was not there although sometime he worked with Ralph Morgan's orchestra. I worked the "big room" with Henny Youngman, Slapsy Maxie Rosenbloom, and many others. I used to perform in my shows and then go upstairs and sing with Jack on dance sets. I had a lot of fun in those days and Jack and his mother took me to visit all the fantastic places.

Home Again

My new agent had me get new pictures from a professional photographer. I used the new photographs to make table tents. It was great for me because on the back of the picture there was a blank post card. I would tell my audiences that if they wanted to know where I would be playing or when I would be back to the location they were at if they filled in the information on the postcard and gave it to me or the person who seated them I would mail it back to them and let them know my itinerary. It worked wonders for me because when they would bring me back I would have a packed house!!! The other way the card worked for me was when people who would want to book me or have a business deal would send me the post cared as well. Those post cards helped me a great deal!!!

With my new agent, I started working mostly hotels and very nice supper clubs. My agent decided that I should be working my way out to the west. I told my agent that I had to go home first for one week. I had promised my dad; so I flew back to Akron. By then they had bought 15 acres of land and a nice home out quite away from Akron called Bath, Ohio. I loved it.

LOIS PHILLIPS
"Personality Plus"

LOIS PHILLIPS — A RARE COMBINATION OF DANCING AND POWERHOUSE SONG MATERIAL — HAS LEFT HER MARK OF PRESTIGE ON ALL HER RECENT ENGAGEMENTS. FOLLOWING A TWELVE MONTH TOUR OF THE LEADING NITE SPOTS AND HOTELS ALL OVER THE U.S.A. AND CANADA. HER DANCING AND SINGING DELIGHTED AUDIENCES IN DETROIT — CLEVELAND — CANADA — AND HAS GAINED A REPUTATION OF HOLD-OVER BOOKINGS. BEAUTIFULLY GOWNED — EXCITING PERSONALITY — PLUS A TREMENDOUS REPERTOIRE OF SPECIAL MATERIAL.

MOSS PHOTO SERVICE INC., 350 WEST 50TH STREET, N.Y.C. • PLAZA 7-3520

Dear _____

I saw **LOIS PHILLIPS** tonight — It was a great show.

Love,

P. S.

PLACE STAMP HERE

Lois Phillips

★   ★

WILL BE HAPPY TO AUTOGRAPH
THIS PHOTO FOR YOU

★

ALWAYS A GREAT
SHOW AT THE

Mom & Bob   Ron, Bob, Bill & Mom

They had a horse by the name of Rebel and of course a German shepherd by the name of Atlas whom I became very fond of. My father made him stay outside and every morning he would be at my window looking in when I woke. I had a great week with Ron, Bob, my mom and dad and Rebel, (who I fed apples to when he begged for them at the fence) and of course the shepherd.

My dad decided while I was there that it was time for me to get a car. I called my agent and asked if he could postpone my trip out west and get me something closer to home because I was getting a car. He said everyone wanted me back down South so I told him to book what he could. I had taken drivers training in school but I had to really brush up because I hadn't done that for a while. We went shopping for a car and after looking at quite a few I decided to buy a Cutlass Oldsmobile. They didn't have the interior color of purple that I wanted but my dad ordered me one with all the things on it he thought I should have on the road. I could not get it before I had to go to work so I just decided to work a month or so and then fly back and get my car.

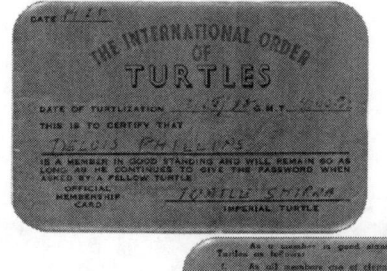

The last night that I was home my father invited our new neighbors over to meet me. They were a lot of fun and that is where I got an invitation to the Turtle Club. It was a fun club and there were several questions you had to answer to get into it; and then when you became a turtle and someone asked you if you were one, you had to say "You bet your sweet ass I am!" So being a new "turtle" I took my card with me.

On Tour

The next day I flew into Louisville Kentucky to work at the Iroquois Supper Club. The owner was excited to have me back and I had a wonderful two weeks. My dad phoned me and said that my car was there so I told the owner that I could only work one more week because I had to fly back home and get my car. He told me to keep in touch and I could work there anytime I wanted. I flew back to Ohio. My dad picked me up at the airport and took me to the parking lot where he handed me a set of keys and pointed to a white cutlass Oldsmobile that had a purple ribbon tied around it!!! I was so thrilled; I cried and hugged my dad. He said he tried to get a purple interior (my favorite color) but the only color he thought I might like that they had was red. It was beautiful.

It was beginning to be winter and it was snowing and Bath was beautiful. My dad had taken care of everything I needed on my car including snow tires. My agent called and he said he was putting the west coast on hold because they were all asking for me back in Florida. I asked him if he could break my jump for me since I was now driving so he started booking me in the south again.

I went to Memphis, Baton Rouge, Louisiana and back to Nashville. When I would go to Nashville I always did a show for the care center there that had little kids with no homes and were injured. There was one that I loved, he was a little boy with no legs and no arms, I would always sing to him and he would call me his girlfriend. I used to get as many of the entertainers I could round up to do a show there and the house band I was working with would always go play for it.

—Staff Photo by Jack Gunter

SUMMER PARTY — Lynn Ashworth, Nettie Johnson and Mary Barton (front) were among the youngsters at Junior League Home for Crippled Children entertained Friday by dancer Marie Leslie, singer Lois Phillips, The Ike Cole Trio, emcee David (Deadeye) Schulman, and comedians Ronny Beck and Frank Link. The two-hour performance is an annual late-summer party arranged by Schulman. It also served as "going-away" salute to Home administrator Gene Clark, who is moving to St. Louis. He has been succeeded as of today by William H. Pigg.

Well one time after I had rounded up all the entertainers, the house band they had said they wouldn't do it unless they got paid. I told them that no one got paid we all did it for the kids. I was so upset, it was two days before we were supposed to perform so that night after I got through working I went down to the Black Poodle lounge to "drown my sorrows" and I was telling the bartender what had happened, there was a band playing but I was so upset, here I had all those entertainers set to entertain and no band, that I didn't even hear them.

33

Shortly after I told my sad story I got a tap on my shoulder from a tall black man who introduced himself as Ike Cole. I was so excited to meet Nat's brother. I knew Nat from working with him on a gig. He told me that he overhead me and would be happy to donate his guys with him to help me out. I was thrilled!! So we did the show and it went great and Ike even bought the children toys!!! What a great guy he was!

Then a big step came when I was booked into the Crushendow in Los Angeles. I was excited because I was booked there with Lenny Bruce a well-known comic at that time. I was not so excited with him after I worked with him. Lenny was on drugs and sometimes I would have to do extra time on the show for him to get ready to do his spot. He was probably the only entertainer I worked with that I really didn't care for; I did have a great deal of fun with the band and was held over for another two weeks after Lenny left as the headliner.

Then a couple by the name of Joe and Marilyn Hooven wrote some cute special material songs for me and helped me put together an act. I loved LA. I had an apartment at 10600 Wilshire Boulevard and had such a good time!

Then MCA out of New York heard about me and they started booking me in the hotels in Miami. You used to be able to do one night shows at different hotels up and down the beach and that was always great. I had to have 20 piece arrangements made because I was working with so many different musicians. I was doing so good I was asked to headline some of the shows. I had a great deal of excitement in Florida and thought I would like to live there one day.

My agent then booked me at the Galt Ocean Mile in Ft. Lauderdale, Florida, and I was there when a hurricane came through. Where I was working in the lounge when you were up on stage you could see into the lobby which had windows all over the front. I was told to keep the audience watching me as the weather got worse outside. I did real well until while I was singing on stage and I saw a tree come through the window in the front of the hotel at which point I told everyone let's all have a Drink!!!! It was really frightening that whole evening. We were without electricity and it was really scary. You could see cars pass by the window with big palm trees behind them, it was no fun! The next day we were still without electricity but as the day went on it got better.

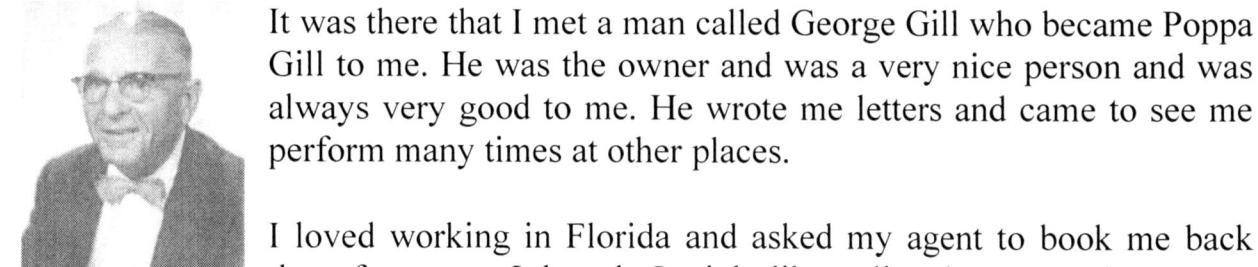

It was there that I met a man called George Gill who became Poppa Gill to me. He was the owner and was a very nice person and was always very good to me. He wrote me letters and came to see me perform many times at other places.

I loved working in Florida and asked my agent to book me back there for a year. I thought I might like to live there someday. It was so much fun you could work a different hotel every night and sometimes get to see other entertainers. Back in those days all of the old entertainers got along so well another singer would come in and I would let them get up a do a song, if I needed lyrics to a song or they needed lyrics to a song we always shared. It was fun helping each other and meeting so many nice people and working with so many bands. Charlie Spivack's music he did for me plus all the other musicians I worked with really came in handy! The only thing I didn't like about it was the humidity and the bugs. (The "no see-ums" and the big roaches called palmetto bugs). It was those things and the humidity that made me decide not to live in Florida!

From there it was Christmas time and I always tried to get home on Christmas so I got into my car and drove. I got home at around 3:00 in the morning and my dad was waiting for me with a fire in the fireplace and hot buttered rum. It was that night that I thanked my dad for all he did for me. I told him how mean I thought he was when he made me work and learn all the things I did. He said "you have no idea how hard it was for me to be so hard on you but I wanted you to learn so badly and I loved you so much!!" He was the only "Dad" I really had and I always felt so lucky to have him. Christmas at our house was always fun and special. Even with all my travels I always tried to make it home for the Christmas holiday.

೦ Cruising

After Christmas I was back to work again and this time went to Florida to work on a cruise line. The name of the ship was the Franca C. It was a fun "gig" I worked the first night out and the last night in and the rest of the time I was just like all of the travelers. I was excited and kind of frightened, I had never been on an ocean liner before and I was to work there a whole week. Everyone was wonderful to me my first day. I got to meet my band and rehearse with them. They were all Italian and really great. There was a brother team on the show and a comic. As a headliner, I had to close it and I really had a good time.

Today's Events

Monday, April 1, 1963

Welcome to Curaçao, N.A.

6:30	9:30 a.m.	Breakfast in the Dining Room
6:30	10:30 a.m.	Continental breakfast served in cabins
7:00 a.m.		Ms. Franca C. is due to arrive at Curaçao
		Taxies are available along shipside.
10:45 a.m.		Bouillon served — Sun deck
12:30	1:30 p.m.	Luncheon

ALL ABOARD!

1:45 p.m. — Please allow at least 45 minutes for return to the ship in the event that the Pontoon Bridge is open. There is free ferry-service if the bridge is open.

2:00 p.m.	Ms. FRANCA C. sails for Port-au-Prince, Haiti, (638 seamiles)
4:30 5:00 p.m.	Afternoon Tea — Ballroom
5:00 p.m.	Italian Class by Maria Pia — Chapel
5:30 p.m.	Holy Mass — Lounge
7:00 8:00 p.m.	Cocktail time. Music.
7:30 8:30 p.m.	Dinner — Lounge
9:00 p.m.	BINGO. Try the whims of lady luck!

SHOW TIME

9:00 p.m. 1st performance	Lois Phillips	Bob Baxter	Ramon and Lucinda	The Lyric Twins
10:15 p.m. 2nd performance		Ray Kidd M.C.		Ballroom

Dancing follows — Lounge

11:20 p.m. — Light buffet

12:00 Midnite — Shall we carry on in the Nite Club.

Please turn over

So that you know something about the artists appearing here tonight...

Ray Kidd - Your singing Cruise Director
Ray, born in Pittsburgh, commenced his formal education at Duquesne University in Pennsylvania, continuing at Miami University. His flair for show business, along with undisputable talent has taken him with 28 touring major Broadway musical productions such as "Call Me Madame", and "Carousel". Ray was feature vocalist for 2 months with the world-famed "Folies Bergère" of Paris, culminated from his extensive world tours. Ray has literally "sung his way around the world". Space here precludes elaborating, however, we feel his European engagements, including the Hilton Hotels is worthy of mention. Mr. Kidd recently combined his vocal talents with Cruise Activities and is happy to be beginning his third season with the Atlantic Cruise Line. Making his home in Miami, however seldom there, Ray expects to devote all efforts to cruising for the immediate future.

Lois Phillips
A young and personable singer who is a member of a lost art: "Soubrette". Lois has appeared in Los Angeles, Miami Beach, Nevada and far off Alaska. We are happy to welcome her on her first Cruise Ship, the "Franca C".

Ramon and Lucinda
Our Latin American dancing stars wish to share with you their world experience of dancing happiness for you to enjoy now, and in your future dancing pleasure. Their great talent, charm and sincerely has won them numerous friends.
P.S. - They know the Caribbean area well and will tell.

The Lyric Twins
England's musical comedy, novelty team. They were educated on the Continent and featured at the leading supper clubs and theatres of Europe. This included the London Palladium, the famed Astor Club, plus T.V. appearances in England and U.S.A. They now make their home in Miami appearing in season at top beach hotels as Carillon, Deluxe etc.

Bob Baxter
Started at 15 in show business working at a Carnival as a fire-eater, later branched into jugeling then mastered the art of magic performing these various talents with a sense of comedy. Bob recently played the Play-boy Club Circuit with a comedy routine and pantomine. He just concluded an engagement at the Intercontinental Hotel at Curaçao. He has played all over Europe and Australia.

GIACOMO COSTA FU ANDREA - GENOVA

Mv. Franca C.

THE LYRIC TWINS

36

The first night out is always rough on the water so that is why they always had a show going out to sea and coming back in. I remember half way through my show the ship started to move from side to side and I ended up in some guys lap, of course being an entertainer I had a lot of fun out of that and so did the audience! The guys in the band were wonderful to me. I told them I was going to Spain to entertain and that I was hoping to learn a song in Spanish. I always tried to learn a song in the language of the places I went out of respect for their country. The guys in the band told me they had one that I would love. I found out that Italian and Spanish were very close so they helped me with the words. It was a beautiful song called *Historia de Amour*. I still sing it today.

I would go into the dining room in the morning and they would be sitting there and they would make me sing the lyrics to them so I could learn it correctly. I became very close to the leader and he wrote me several letters and we kept in touch for quite some time. I also received letters from one of the brothers from the dance team. I made a lot of friends and I came back and worked on the ship three more times.

When I came back to Florida I got to work Cape Canaveral and I got to meet the astronauts. They came into the hotel I was working and I was invited to have a drink at their table. We had great fun talking and I introduced them to my Turtle Club from Ohio and they got a big kick out of it so I made them all turtles. We had so much fun together and when Wally Shiarra went up into space after that one of the other guys asked him if he was a turtle and he answered "you bet your sweet ass I am" and all the reporters tried to erase that part!

Winnipeg Visitors Guide

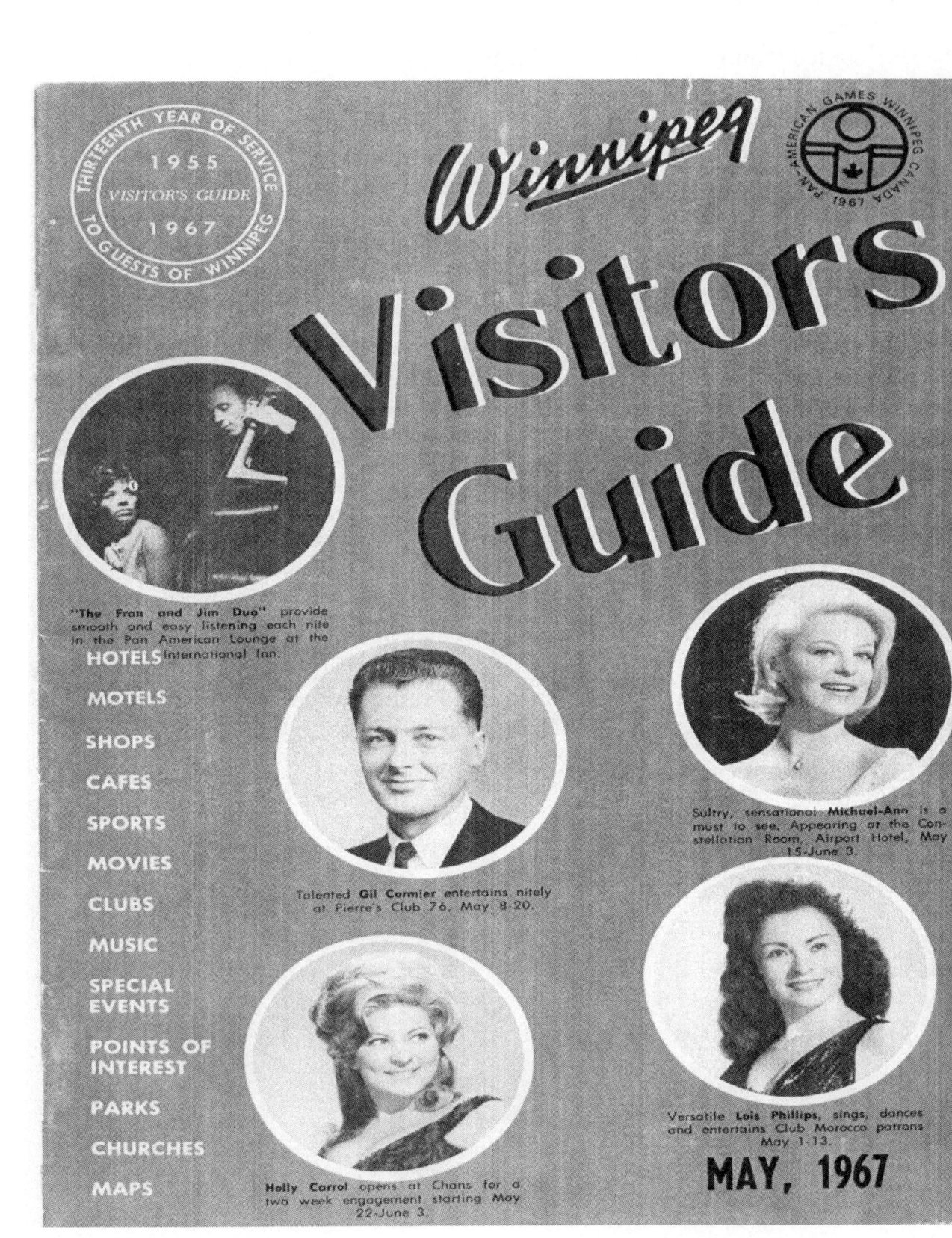

MAY, 1967

THIRTEENTH YEAR OF SERVICE TO GUESTS OF WINNIPEG
1955 VISITOR'S GUIDE 1967

PAN-AMERICAN GAMES WINNIPEG CANADA 1967

- HOTELS
- MOTELS
- SHOPS
- CAFES
- SPORTS
- MOVIES
- CLUBS
- MUSIC
- SPECIAL EVENTS
- POINTS OF INTEREST
- PARKS
- CHURCHES
- MAPS

"The Fran and Jim Duo" provide smooth and easy listening each nite in the Pan American Lounge at the International Inn.

Talented **Gil Cormier** entertains nitely at Pierre's Club 76, May 8-20.

Sultry, sensational **Michael-Ann** is a must to see. Appearing at the Constellation Room, Airport Hotel, May 15-June 3.

Holly Carrol opens at Chans for a two week engagement starting May 22-June 3.

Versatile **Lois Phillips**, sings, dances and entertains Club Morocco patrons May 1-13.

ᛞ Off Shore

In my career most of my overseas traveling was for the Sheraton and the Hilton Hotels. When I was in Canada, I was in Winnipeg and Edmonton. Learning everyone's customs and way of life was very educational and has helped me in my life understanding people because of knowing their customs and how they lived. It gives you depth in knowing why people react the way they do.

I got to go to Hong Kong and I was tickled because in those days you could buy sequin gowns there very cheap and jewelry so of course I purchased quite a few things that I loved there. Men would go there to buy suits very cheap at that time. It was a great place to pick up a lot of different things cheaper than you could buy them in the states.

My next stop was Rome. I loved Italy, it was beautiful and the people were fun to be around, the men were very romantic and the scenery was wonderful, I loved the music and the people were very nice to me.

In the middle of those times I got to travel to Damascus, Syria, Greece and I fell in love with belly dancing there. One of my friends from this country was born there and when I worked there he came to see me. He took me down to the clubs and I got to see belly dancing.

I wanted to learn belly dancing so he arranged to have a car pick me up after I got through singing at the hotel and take me down to the club where a woman taught me to belly dance. After I learned the dance, they thought I should perform at the club. They told me not to talk so that people would think I was from their country and they gave me the nickname of Nuedemia. I had long hair at the time and when I was singing I would wear it up then I would brush it down in the car on my way to the club and change into a costume and dance.

I was taught a number that a woman dances when she becomes betrothed. She starts to dance and all the family and friends make a big circle and however well she dances determines how much money she gets for her dowry. You bend back towards the audience and they stick bills in your bra, not in a fresh way and sometimes in your skirt. It was one of those times that my agent came in from New York to see me and asked me to go out with him that night, I didn't want him to know I was working after hours at the club so I told him I had plans. I went down to the club as usual and while I was working that night I bent back while I was dancing and saw him sitting at a table looking at me, He then yelled, "keep it in the act." I didn't want him to know I was making more money in my bra there than singing at the hotel!!

I went to Madrid, Spain and had a wonderful time there, it was great everywhere. I wanted to learn their customs and the dances of each place. I found the Spanish men very romantic. They would sing to you under your balcony. I was having a wonderful time and was very intrigued by the Spanish men....Then my agent came over and took me to a bullfight; I thought it was going to be just like I had seen on TV but only the first part of it was like that with the parades etc. The matador dedicated the bull to me and I was thrilled, but not for long. I didn't realize they stuck swords in it before the bullfighter was there; I couldn't help from feeling sorry for the bull. When he killed the bull he cut off his ear and put it on a velvet pillow and presented it to me. My agent told me to smile but I thought I was going to throw up) Needless to say it was not something I ever wanted to relive again!!! Even though I dated the bullfighter and he gave me his hat (which I still have) I decided I definitely did not want to see a real bullfight again. Although years later I made up a tap number with a cape etc. like the bullfight.........

When I worked the Upside Down Hilton in San Juan, Porto Rico I had wonderful time and was very spoiled by my customers that came in for my show. The bullfighter from Madrid found out I was there and he surprised me. He took me to a lot of places to see and we had a great time! The owner of the lounge took us for tours and the people were helpful and full of fun. I danced in the streets with all of the people that did that just like I did in Spain and Hawaii, and sang my *Historia De Amour*.

I also got to go to Hawaii. I worked a hotel called the Royal Hawaiian. I really enjoyed it so much there and the people were great to me. While I was there I got to travel all over Hawaii. I loved the scenery and the people. I learned the hula and Tahitian dancing while I was there from a very nice lady that I met. Tahitian was very difficult you had to keep your feet flat on the floor and with all the movements of the hips that was not easy! As I traveled to so many places I got to know the people and their customs. I danced with them around the fires at night, it was great...I think that helps you understands people and what they do and say when you know their background. If it had not been so humid there I am sure that would have been one of the places I would have liked to live.

The next time I had a booking there my mother wanted to go to Hawaii and I called the people I was working for and they told me to come in a week before I started working there and they would give me a room "on the house" since I was bringing my mother there. The first day we arrived she was so excited, Virginia Bradley's husband had passed away and she wanted to come with us. We all had a great time on the plane. When we arrived and got to the hotel we walked into the room and they had a bottle of my mother's favorite scotch and my favorite (at that time) VO and two bottles of my favorite Asti Spumante. When I saw that I now understood why they asked me what my Mom liked to drink, I knew they all knew what I drank! I took mom and our friend Virginia all over the island and they really had a great time. I even took them to Maui. The next week I had to work (which to me was always and still is my "fun.")

Then I got to go to Paris. I was so thrilled I wrote to my friend Maggi Orsoni in Lyon and told her I was going there. She wrote me back and told me she would come on my day off and bring me to Lyon.

When I was in school and studying French you were given pen pals. You wrote to them in French and they were to write to you in English. We had kept in touch all those years and I was thrilled to finally meet her. It was a wonderful experience going to Lyon. It was really beautiful. Paris was interesting and it was great to see all that I got to see.

I wasn't so tickled to when you went to the bathroom, they had them on the streets and people could look over the top of the little stalls and talk to you……It was not the cleanest place I had been either and many of ladies used perfume instead of bathing a lot. I still remembered some of my French from school so I did get to talk to a lot of the locals. I met different kinds of men everywhere I went. I learned a lot from all my travels to so many beautiful places I got to visit.

❧ Stateside Again

Then I was booked in Alaska for the armed forces and air force bases. I worked in Anchorage and Fairbanks. The Anchorage soldiers were great to work for and I had a great time. One of the airmen's clubs didn't have a mike or anything but being taught to entertain regardless I had them put a spotlight on a stack of beer boxes and I sang and danced for all of them. One of the captains took me for breakfast and ordered me moose milk. I thought it was a breakfast drink and really enjoyed it but by the time breakfast came out I wasn't sure I could see it much less eat it. The moose milk had about three different kinds of booze in it but it kind of tasted like chocolate I guess from the Kahlua but of course I drank it. At the end of my run when I was put on the plane the guys all got together and voted me the girl they would like to go on survival training with!! I had a lot of laughs with that one!!! I have to admit they spoiled me and I had a lot of fun working for the air force and armed force bases.

When I went back to the states I went back to working all over the south and Florida then I ran into Jack again. We started dating again and this time he wanted to get married but I was honest with him and told him I was having such a good time working that I wasn't ready to get married. So he told me to keep in touch with him and if I got close to Seattle let him know because he and his mother were living there and he wanted me to meet her, so I told him I would.

It was shortly after that that I got an offer to go back out west again; so of course I did. I was again at Portland; and Jack bought his mother there to meet me. She was so sweet and great to be around!! He called her the "Mouse."

She had been in vaudeville as a dancer and his dad was a comic. Jack started performing with them when he was 5 years old. I loved Mouse. When I met her she was 82 and drank martinis every night! She called that her brightener. She and I got along very well; I got a big kick out of her.

Jack had to go back to Seattle for a few days so Mouse stayed with me, I found out she carried this great big old fashioned gun with her for her safety. I took her to the club with me and sat her at the bar, she knew no strangers and if a guy asked to buy her a drink she would look at him and say she could afford to buy her own drink!!! The night that Jack got back after the show he walked mouse to her room and came back to the bar where he and I had a drink, we were talking when all of a sudden we heard police sirens, and a bunch of noise, we left the bar and went back towards Mouse's room and cops were all over the place. We got there just in time to find out that some guy came into the room and she thought it was Jack so she said "Is that you Jack?" and she said he answered yes and she knew it wasn't him so she got out her gun and shot at him. I guess he ran out of the room and someone called the police. She told the cop that the guy lied to her so she tried to shoot him. I know it wasn't funny but I couldn't help but laugh. She was a brave little lady. After my gig I took a few days and went to Jack's house in Seattle and stayed with him and his mother. Every night there was cocktail time!!!

❧ Showbusiness

❧ Showtime

I talked to Jack and told him I decided to get a band of my own to back me. One of my agents thought that would be a good idea. When I started interviewing guys I told them at the beginning that if I caught any of them on drugs or if they came in drunk or they started messing around with any of the girls that worked where we working I would fire them. So many of the times the owners of places were going with the waitress, etc. and there would be real trouble for everyone involved in the band if one of them would be caught with the boss's girlfriend.

I found a great piano man by the name of Milt Raymond. He was with Ozzie and Harriet when they were entertainers. My drummer I found was a funny little guy by the name of Jimmy and a great horn player and bass player. My first "gig" with them was in Florida. We worked a lot of the hotel lounges and one night a guy by the name of Burt Stevens came in and after staying most of the evening watching three of my shows offered me a job at the Boca Raton Hotel and Club in Boca Raton, Florida. He wanted me to do a dance set and a show set all night long like I was doing there. I gave him the name of my agent and told him to call him and I was sure he could arrange it.

WEDNESDAY, FEBRUARY 26, 1964

Boca Raton
HOTEL AND CLUB

Proudly Presents

Jack La Delle

Lois Phillips

Patio Royale - 10:00 P.M.

Formal Attire Required

(Cathedral Dining Room
will be open
for Informal Dining)

Dancing
to Claude Thornhill's Orchestra

Call Ken - Ext. 84
for Reservations

HOTEL AND CLUB
Boca Raton, Florida

Cabana Sun Club
With the azure South Atlantic as a backdrop, and a quarter mile of unbroken white sand and surf as your own private beach, there is nothing in the serene sweep of the tropics to compare with the magnificent Cabana Sun Club at Boca Raton.

I was booked there for two weeks and they kept picking up my option and I ended up being there one year. Many very important people came in there, politicians, actors, etc. I loved it there and they gave me a beautiful apartment on the beach. One of the special moments I had was one night we saw that Vaughn Monroe was booked in the big room. I was so excited, I had told the guys about working with him on a show and how nice he was to me so they told me that I should go say hello to him and I said he wouldn't remember me, that was so long ago and only one show. We were rehearsing in the afternoon when I told them that and shortly after those words came out of my mouth I heard a familiar voice say "Where is that redhead?" It was Vaughn! I was so thrilled. He was with my boss and he invited me to sit in the front row while he did his show, I looked at my boss and he gave me the OK. Needless to say it was a wonderful night. I got to work with him later
On.

When Vaughn left I asked him to give some friends of mine a call that lived in Port St. Lucie as he was going through there on his way home. They loved him and they called me a day after he left and said that he did in fact stop by their house. He rang the doorbell and when they opened it he stood there with a bottle of booze in

his hand and said DeLois told me that if I stopped here with a bottle of booze you would invite me in for a drink!!! They were thrilled and I got a big kick out of it! He was a great guy!

On March 15th, my birthday I got several surprises while I was working there. I had many good times at the Boca, and on that night I was given a whole case of Lancers Portuguese wine (my favorite in those days). Then after the show my guys and I went down to the little bar we always went to after work and the guys in my band had a surprise party for me. All of my regulars at Boca were there and I had a birthday drink with all of them!! When it was time to leave my guys in the band followed me outside (they had planned to drive me home) but I asked the cops to take me, I told them that I was too drunk to drive. I laughed at myself the next morning when I woke up on my couch with my mink coat still around my shoulders and my car keys in my hand!!!

Jack came to visit me from time to time on the road and he really got to like my guys so well he booked us on several shows with him. Always loving to headline I let him. I didn't care as long as I could entertain!! We worked all over Florida, sometimes without Jack as he was still working as a solo most of the times

In the Intimate Salon Rouge

★

Don't Miss
JACK LA DELLE
and
LOIS PHILLIPS

★

JOIN THE LIVELY ONES... FUN... DANCING...
TWO SHOWS NIGHTLY AT 9 & 11 (except Mondays)...
GOURMET DINNERS FROM $3.25... NOW SERVING OUR
FAMOUS KEY LIME PIE... MAKE RESERVATIONS NOW!

GUY LOMBARDO'S

Port-O-Call

MOTOR HOTEL AND ISLAND RESORT
On The Beautiful Islands Of
TIERRA VERDE

At **Port-O-Call** the big entertainment package in the **Salon Rouge** is supplied by **Jack La Delle** and his talented show group. Sparkler in this group is **Lois Phillips** a pert little song and dance gal who really rates all the applause she gets. Lois works the audience beautifully with a cute number, "Gimme a Little Mink" and shows off her terpsichorean talents in a Hawaiian number and a dazzling bullfight sequence both highlighted by the unusual effects of blacklight. Versatile is the best word to describe Jack La Delle as he happily combines his talents as m.c., comic and musician. Jack plays a total of 32 instruments and it looks as though he hauled most of them into Port-O-Call. Ensemble numbers by the group have a big band sound that make them highly danceable. A plush spot for an evening of dining, dancing and entertainment.

I had some wonderful memories everywhere I went. If I told you all of my wonderful memories my book would be about 5,000 pages long. I got to work with people like Jerry Lester, Jerry Van Dyke, Vaughn Monroe, Johnny Desmond, and Don Rickles, Don used to come out after I got through performing and say after watching me he felt as sexy as a stuffed olive!!!

MON., APRIL 19, 1971 — Columbus Dispatch 21B

De Lois and Company Blockbuster at Boehm

By JAMES BRADSHAW
Of The Dispatch Staff

Stemming from both hemispheres, songs from the deep south to New York's west side, a touch of Syrian belly dancing, stroboscopic and ultraviolet lighting effects...

No, it's not an extravaganza (at least in size). It's the regular, fast-moving act of Miss De Lois and Her Men, performing nightly through Saturday at the Boehm Haus, 165 N. Murray Hill Rd.

MISS DE LOIS certainly is not new to Columbus, and her skits are certain to insure her return, but for those who haven't seen her, she's a petite West Virginia gal who started her show business career by dancing and never has stopped.

(If you catch her not moving, report to the management — it's probably a breach of contract).

She has added to her footwork what is probably one of the most pleasant, controlled and versatile voices on the night scene.

The "Down Home" flavor of her origins comes through early in country and western numbers such as "I Didn't Promise You A Rose Garden," or "A Little Bitty Tear."

AT OTHER times, she is a sultry siren ("I'm A Woman"), a hip chick ("Knock Three Times"), a Broadway nut ("Everything's Comin' Up Roses") or the impersonator of adolescent age ("Jeepers Creepers").

Meanwhile, the special effects go on.

In addition to the lighting variations, there is an effective musical background through the use of tape recordings of "Frankie and Johnie," which is given vocal narration by organist Jim Nells.

Nells also proves he has a presentable voice in a solo of "Go Away, Little Girl."

THE SECOND of "Der Men," Evan Jones, confines himself to the drums, but doesn't confine his drums at all, as evidenced in "When the Saints Go Marchin' In."

The lilt of "I'm Leavin' On a Jet Plane" brings to mind Columbus' loss and Indianapolis' gain as Miss De Lois moves on to her next engagement after Saturday.

Val Boehm's supper club forerunner was the Ramblewood West.

De Lois Phillips ... One would think ... *Our DeLois Phillips,* the singer who started out from our town as a dancer, was already out West. "Miss De Lois and Her Men" are at the Ciulleoni's Restaurant — but it's in Indianapolis... She seems to be picking up momentum. In an appearance at the Boehm Haus in Columbus, the former Ramblewood West, she drew from the Dispatch one of the most enthusiastic reviews of a night club act we've ever read... She's the daughter of Mrs. W. W. Evans, 1684 Squirrel rd.

NOW APPEARING AT THE TOWN HOUSE SUPPER CLUB

CHARLIE SPIVAK
and His Famous Band

Co-Starring
LOIS PHILLIPS
(Personality Plus)
Two Shows Nitely

Langford HOTEL
Winter Park
RESERVATIONS MI 7-3100

NIGHTERS, Restaurants

Sunday, January 5, 1964

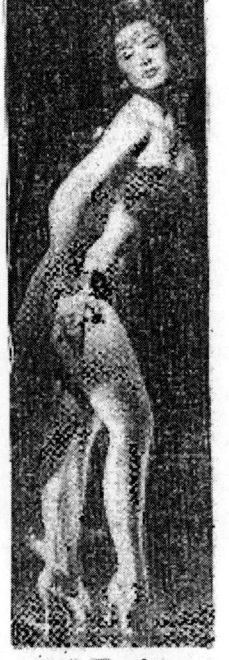

Will Perform In Musical

Shapely Lois Phillips is a member of the chorus in "Guys and Dolls" Broadway musical which will open the summer season of the Miami Music Theater July 15.

Wednesday, July 31, 1963

Dear Guest:

For your entertainment pleasure this evening, we are pleased to present our "GALA COMPLIMENTARY SHOW AND DANCE" in the LA RONDE ROOM at 9:30 P.M.

Starring in this exciting show will be BOYLAN & WALL, LOIS PHILLIPS, ELIZABETH & LEE, ZIGGY LANE, your Singing-Host, and the music of LENNY DAWSON'S ORCHESTRA.

Admission will be by tickets which may be obtained by presenting your room key or cabana card at the Social Desk in the South Lobby from 5:30 - 9:30 P.M. this evening; and reservations are suggested by calling LA RONDE.

We wish you a pleasant evening.

ZIGGY LANE
Host-Director of Entertainment

DON HALL'S Esquire Dinner Club

proudly presents the

JACK LA BELLE SHOW
with
LOIS PHILLIPS

Jack and Lois have just finished six weeks with the Wayne King Band.

Jack is a genial multi-talented leader-musician who battles his audience by switching from trumpet to alto sax, tenor sax, and soprano sax to trumpet, mandolin, clarinet, Hawaiian guitar and steel guitar, to clarinet and then tunes in a Como style ballad. His accomplishments include playing with Harry James, Tommy Dorsey and the Jack La Belle Musical Scrapbook on NBC.

Petite and lovely Lois Phillips will drive you mad with her exotic Egyptian belly dance, her tantalizing Cat Girl Act, her romantic South Sea Island Hula and Rudolph the Red Nose Reindeer dance... all in black light. Lois is one of the most lovely and versatile girls in show business today. Lois can sing in several languages that excite the pulse beat of the Gay's garden. Plus singing with the Wayne King Band, Lois has sung with Vaughn Monroe and Guy Lombardo.

The Jack La Belle show is backed by three superb musicians playing your favorite dinner and dance music. Come out and see the Jack La Belle Show with Lois Phillips, including a top musical group with a real "big band" sound.

Three floor shows nightly. If you haven't made your Christmas party reservations yet, please do so. The finest in food, atmosphere, congeniality and good clean family type entertainment. Honoring American Express, Diner's Club and Hilton Carte Blanche credit cards.

Still serving delicious tacos from 5 to 7 p.m. Also Lola Eatery Menu which includes our famous French Dipped Prime Rib Sandwich. No prices over $1.95. Also our regular menu with 21 taste tingling entrees and 21 ala carte items.

EVERGLADES

NOW!
MISS DELOIS
and her
MUSIC MEN

Sonny Jones & Peller Oriental Dancer

NO COVER
NO MINIMUM
4250 W. Broad
274-0500

The Biloxi-Gulfport Daily Herald—12
Friday Afternoon, August 19, 1966

Now! — Through Aug. 21

Pictured Above: Jerry Van Dyke, well received by Ed Sullivan.

JERRY VAN DYKE
Star of television show "My Mother The Car" and many television appearances and some movies.

LOIS PHILLIPS
Talented vocalist, dancer ... presents Latin American coming from Miami.

Don Sanders
Comedian and M.C.

MIKE SERPAS AND HIS BAND
for your dancing pleasure.

Plenty of Room For Everyone. No Reservations Needed . . . Come As You Are.

Coffee Shop and Dining Room Separate from Supper Club ...
Serving A Family Budget Menu.

Breakfast	50¢
Luncheon	90¢
8-Oz. Fillet Wrapped In Bacon, Baked Potato w/Sour Cream	2.50
Delicious Shish Kebab (marinated in sauce and wine served flaming at your table) Chef salad and baked potato	3.25
Assorted Child's Plate	90¢
AFTER CHURCH SUNDAY SPECIAL Baked Chicken & Dressing, Chefs Salad, Green Peas	$1.25

OPEN 24 HOURS DAILY

GUS STEVENS
On The Beach
Highway 90,
Biloxi

COAST WIZ

VOLUME I

NO. 18

AUGUST 19, 1966

51

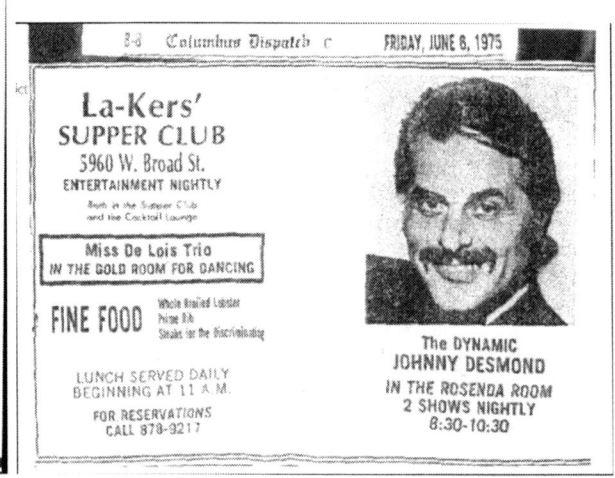

September 13, 1973 - ROCKY FORK ENTERPRISE - Page 3

CORRECTION

Earl Walker's name was spelled incorrectly in last week's paper, and we take this opportunity to spell it correctly. Mr. Walker, 9490 Havens Corner Rd. is one of five candidates running for Jefferson Township Trustee.

HUNTERS RIDGE

Continued from Page 1

"first shopping center in Ohio". He said, the aim is to "get the cooperation of the tenant and the city fathers, and produce something that is a credit to the community". Black added, "one of our partners is Nicholas Sage, a resident of Gahanna."

| THE RIGHT WAY | UN-ENDORSED UN-PARTISAN UN-COMMITTED |

CAST UN VOTE FOR

ERNEST M. STRAUSS

Pd. Pol. Adv. By Candidate For Council

Country & Western Weekend

FRI. & SAT. SEPT. 14-15

NEW COLONY LABEL — RECORDING STAR

Miss De Lois Lounge
155 Mill St.
(Plenty of Parking in Back)

Miss DeLois and The Park Ave. Hillbillies

ALSO **SQUARE DANCE** SUNDAY

"GOOD OLD FASHION FUN"

Holiday Inn OF AMERICA

LAST WEEK TO HEAR MISS DE LOIS & MEN IN LOUNGE

Debut for Country and Western. This weekend will be Country and Western's debut at the Miss Delois Lounge. DeLois Phillips, co-owner of the lounge with Bonnie Evans, is standing by the juke box playing her first recording, featuring her rendition of "Country Road" and "Daddy was a preacher, but Momma was a go-go girl." Miss DeLois and The Park Ave. Hillbillies will be featured for the country weekend. Bob Weber will also be adding his talents and will be the caller for the old fashion square dance to be held Sunday evening. Miss DeLois's credits include over three years of singing on a worldwide tour to such places as Damascus, Madrid, and across the Caribbean. She has also worked with Charlie Spivak's band.

The Dunes

(A CHARTERED PRIVATE CLUB)

Open Nightly For The Fall Season

Shows at 8:30 and 12:30

Unsurpassed Cuisine

LOIS PHILLIPS
Musical Comedy Ballet Tap Dancer

STELLA GARRETT
Reading and TV Singing Star

Another great memory was while I was working the Fontainebleau lounge in Miami and the guys in my band surprised me when they took me into the big room to see Frank.

Sinatra's show and they had him sing happy birthday to me. I was so thrilled he was always one of my favorites!! It was there I met a nice gentleman who had his sons with him. He came in almost every night. He was old enough to be my father and was always very good to me. One night he gave me a beautiful pearl and diamond bracelet. He said he was worried about me being in show business and if I ever needed a ride home I could always cash in the bracelet and get that ticket home. Although I thought it was beautiful, I didn't know it was real. A few years later I loaned it to a friend who lost two of the pearls. I took it to the repair shop and found it to be extremely expensive and probably could have gotten me home from anywhere in the world !My band and I used to do a show set and then a dance set and kept going that way until two o'clock at night. One night while we were playing the dance set and I was in front with the mike singing this guy kept dancing by and feeling my ankle. Well I put up with it for a while and then I announced over the mike looking straight at the guy if he felt my ankle one more time I would hit him over the head with my mike!!! Everyone laughed but his girlfriend, but he didn't touch my ankle again!

I worked for a great guy by the name of Skull Shulman after that. Skull was very good to me and bought me a poodle which I named Mingo. I decided that would be great now that I was going to have a car he could travel with me. Being a dog lover all my life I fell in love with him immediately. I was afraid that someone might steal him so I tried to train him to stay with me and guard things. Skull and one of his partners owned a lounge called the Black Poodle Lounge. Which my poodle became quite a show himself.

He loved to try to play piano, get on sliding boards, and conning the chefs into giving him food! I would take him to the park and he would stand in line with the kids at the sliding board waiting for his turn, (sometimes cheating)! He loved to swing on the swings and just try everything the little kids did in the park! I laugh at the pictures I took of him. He would always be back stage when we worked. When we played Proud Mary he loved that song and thought he had to dance and "sing" to it. He used to sit in my horn man's case a lot of nights when we did shows. So when I sang that song I would have my horn man take him out then one night I decided to tell the audience about him and I let him show them his "act." Everyone loved it! One night I came up to my hotel room and he had pulled one of my full skirted gowns off the hanger and was lying in the middle of it. He was so funny and wonderful to be with! I did get a little mad at him one night when he ate a whole box of my favorite chocolate turtles!!!!!!!

My Old Kentucky Home—Grand Dad Neely

I decided on one of our trips between gigs to take my band to Granddad Neeley's. They had never been to a holler before and they didn't know what to do when the guy stopped us with a rifle in his hand. He asked me "where are you all going?" I said "I'm DeLois Jean and I am going to see my granddad Clarence Neeley." He said "well honey you go on back and if they ain't there you come back and I'll make you all some dinner!!! "The guys in my band could not get over that and when I drove them back down the long road they were speechless. But when we got there my Granddad welcomed all of them and took them in and fed them. They had never had the kind of food that Aunt Evie served them and when it came time to go not one of them was interested in leaving!!! I kept on traveling and had a wonderful time everywhere I went.

Time to say Good By

Then I received a message from my mom that my dad, Bill had only been given a year to live. The whole side of his face was deformed and he lost his one eye. I immediately took my band and went home to see my dad to cheer him up. I decided I had to go back to Ohio so I could be near him. I gave up the group I had because I knew that Ohio did not pay the kind of money I got them on the road. When I got back home my Mingo got up on my dad's lap and licked him in the face.

⋘ Miss DeLois and the Music Men

I called a local agent that I had wrote and told him I was back and I would be looking for a new band. He said he was happy to have me back and got me a job in Columbus, Ohio singing with a band there for the weekend. He said while I was there I could talk to the bandleader and he could recommend some guys. The bandleader was a guy by the name of Joe Lavinger.

Joe was what we used to call a "funny hat" kind of musician, he played drums but he mostly was just funny. I had a good time working with him, he was always "on" and always fun.

He decided I should go with him while he collected commissions from entertainers for my agent and maybe I could hear some of the guys that were working. We went to several places and then he took me a place that had a rock band playing. The organ man was blind but he was really playing well and somewhat different from a rock musician.

JOE LAVINGER and THE TUNETIMERS
JOHN M. MOORE AGENCY
16 East Broad Street
Columbus 15, Ohio

So I told Joe I liked him and I had a feeling that he knew music and would know standards. Joe bet me that he didn't so I went up to the stand and asked him if he knew *Almost Like Being in Love*. He said he did and he asked if I was a singer; and I told him I was; so he asked me what key I sang it in and handed me the mike and I sang it. The other guys just followed along and then I got a request and sang another.

I was singing with the band the rest of the night which Joe got a big kick out of. Then the owner came over and asked him if I would consider working with the band, Joe told him I was a pretty "pricy" performer and he was not sure I would but he would ask me. Normally I would have said no I wasn't interested in working with a rock band but I really thought Jim Melia, was good and it would give me a chance to see if I could use him so I said yes. So to make a long story short, I worked with the band for two weeks and although it was not my style, I packed the place.

I did get to know Jim and I was thrilled with him, he knew so many songs and really played good. So when I left I told him if he ever needed a "gig" to give me a call that I would love to use him in a group of my own. The owner wanted me to stay but I didn't really enjoy working with a rock band. I kept going places with Joe looking at different piano men and Joe asked me why I didn't talk to Jim but I didn't want to take him from a band if he enjoyed it and it was not nice to steal someone.

So after a couple of weeks I got a call from Jim that the owner was going to let them go in a week and he asked me if I still needed a player I told him I did and called Joe and asked him to find a place and a drummer for me. He found me a drummer and a horn player and once again there was Ms. DeLois and the Music Men.

We started working around Ohio. I worked a lot of little night clubs and a bunch of special one night shows. Then I was booked in a very nice supper club called the Everglades. It was owned by a wonderful little Italian guy by the name of Tony Delawoise. I was booked in for two weeks and was there almost two and a half years. I made some wonderful friends there.

The Everglade, 1x5½ Tues.,—
JULY 2—C-J . . . . —..

EVERGLADES

**NOW!
MISS
DELOIS**
and her
MUSIC MEN
Saucey Songs & Patter
Oriental Dancing
**NO COVER
NO MINIMUM**
4250 W. Broad
274-0500

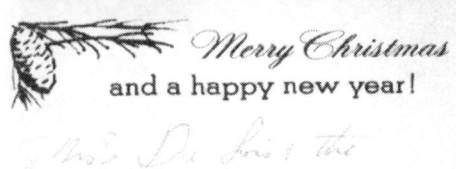

Merry Christmas
and a happy new year!

Dispatch FEATURES

NOW LET ME TELL YOU

Lovely Dancer Stops the Show At Everglades

By JOHNNY JONES

It must be the old showman in me. When I observe the class in entertainment I just want to pass it on. This certainly happened to me the other evening at the Everglades. It was just another evening for dinner at Tony Delewese's place when the time for entertainment came on. Usually chatter boxes, piano players and a singer are the lot today.

The first to catch my eye was Danny Mann with a new set of drums. Danny had the Danny Mann Speakeasy that recently burned out and he is going to open it again soon. Then I noticed Danny leading a blind person to the organ. Jim Melia is his name and you would never know he had been blind from birth. He is truly a fine musician.

Jones

THIS LITTLE combo of Danny and his drums and Melia make music that depends upon excellent rhythm. All these two need is the down beat and they are off.

To the mike came a very attractive young lady, Miss DeLois Phillips. She was born in West Virginia.

How this young lady can belt out songs of every variety. While she was singing out on the floor came Regina McQuay, 7, Tommy, aged 10, and Charles, 10. They live at 27 Olive Ave., Grove City. The family was there for dinner.

Came the rock and roll beat. The youngsters on a corner of the floor and were so good they chased everybody off for a real party. What fun everybody had.

IT WAS TIME for the first show. Miss Phillips then appeared in a stunning sequin Mae West cut-like gown. She was captivating. Then Hawaiian music started and she turned her back to the audience and, with one swish of the zipper, she had stepped out of her sequin gown to display a pretty white skirted Hawaiian outfit. Her interpretation bathed in black light is a work of art.

Then came the last show. She has a little talk about the dances of the East and the many countries she has visited and then does the Dowery dance where the bride dances in the center of a circle of those at her wedding. With this approach she appears in traditional Salome costume. Perhaps outside of Gene Krupa, Danny Mann can hit the skins doing Caravan as well as anybody in the business. Naturally when he has such a fine dancer to accompany the drums play a great part in the dance.

At first I thought this dance of De Lois Phillips another hootch kooch. You feel like apologizing for the thought. Her body control with undulations and arm movements and bumps of the hips is beyond description. It is so lovely the crowd does not wisecrack but succumbs to the dance. It is a long and lovely dance.

I DO NOT BELIEVE even Hinda Wassau, the Queen of Burlesque or the famed Sally Rand could do it as well. Certainly here is a great dancer and singer. And never a dull moment, either.

It was not long until she was brought over to the table. On each table is a nice picture of places she has played. I learned her father is very ill in West Virginia and she is close enough to make frequent visits to see him.

When you can be billed as "Miss Personality Plus" at the famed Boca Raton Hotel and Country Club in Boca Raton, Fla., you are really acceptable any place. The Fountainbleau Hotel in Miami Beach and Sheraton in Chicago have also been on her list.

She really is a powerhouse with her impish grin and sparkling eyes. Certainly Miss DeLois Phillips is a real joy at the Everglades.

I met *Dorothy Walker* one night when she came into the Everglades with several other people. She was very nice and came and told me that they were getting ready to leave and how much she enjoyed my show. She said she probably wouldn't be able to come back because her friends were leaving and she didn't have any more friends that would bring her plus she was going to have to go on dialysis. I felt sorry for her and I said I would pick her up when she wanted to come and she could set at the bar and watch the show. She was so happy. We became good friends and I felt sorry for her because she really had no one; so I would take her to dialysis and then bring her to the Everglades and she would sit at the bar and have fun talking to people and watching the show. I would bring her at least once or twice a week. Then one day she told me she was going to stop dialysis. I told her she couldn't do that she would die if she did. She said she did not want to live the way she lived, she would feel good after dialysis and then she would feel bad again in a day or so and it was like that every time she went. She said she just did not want to spend the rest of her life that way. She did not last long after that and I really cried when I lost her. I had really become good friends and I really hated to lose her…….

Jim Melia, my blind organist, was a nice man. I drove my car pulling his organ on the back of it for our "gigs." Jimmy my drummer was a character, he was a real woman chaser and didn't really have to chase too far. Woman went crazy after musicians. I had the guys working for me quite awhile and a friend of mine from Akron, Linda came to visit me. I introduced her to Jim and they became an item quite quickly. It wasn't long after they met that they married.

When I went back to Nashville and we recorded my "Daddy Was A Preacher" and "Country Road" Jim and I decided to do a number also that Jim wrote the music and I wrote the lyrics. It was called the "Sunnyside of Me" Unfortunately I have not been able to find the record for that. I never had a copy of the written music because Jim was blind, but at least I have the memories. Jim was a very special man and he worked for me a long time.

When I found out I was going to be there longer (I thought a few months at first) I decided to get an apartment instead of staying in a hotel. I looked for a place that would also allow dogs because I had my little Poodle, Mingo. I went shopping for a bed at a furniture store there that Tony recommended and that is where I bought a bed and a round leopard chair. For quite a while that was all I had in my apartment. I have always loved leopard and I was thrilled with the chair (I still have it. I think I was probably the first entertainer to ever wear a leopard gown.

Miss De Lois and her Music Men

We alternated there doing a show set and a dance set from 9:00-2:00. They had wonderful food there and they had a man who parked cars when they came in. We really filled the place.

It is there where I met *Harold and Mary McVay* (who became like a mother and father to me). They had just come back from New Orleans and they said that nothing they saw in New Orleans was as good as my show.

One time when I was in Cincinnati the people I was working for had a party for me on their big boat and Mary and Harold McVay were with me when I went to my party. As we got on the boat I smelled this smell that I will never forget!! Because I used to tell my audiences that I was born in a little town called Sprigg, West Virginia. And I went all the time to visit my other grandddaddy in Tomahawk, Kentucky, who lived in a holler, and of course I explained to my audience what that was. I also told them my grandfather got "White Lightnin" from a lady up on the hill and he used to make everyone take it for snake bits, cold, etc. I used to think it smelled horrible and tasted worse; I tried really hard not to catch a cold so he wouldn't make me to take it. Well, that was the smell when I walked on the boat. The police had confiscated it and they bought it to the party in honor of the "hillbilly." Needless to say we all had a great time!!! I never cared for the "White Lightnin" but the woman up on the hill that made it for my granddad made the best "sippin" whiskey I ever tasted!

After I met the McVays and they had been to the Everglades to see all my shows, they invited me to their house one night. When I went in they took me to their basement and on the way down I looked and on the wall it said Ms. DeLois Lounge with my pictures.

Mr. McVay put a long bar in his basement, a bandstand with an organ, drums, horns and mikes like a professional bandstand and tables and chairs in front of it. It was really fabulous. I can't begin to tell you how many parties we attended down there and how many nights after we got through at the Everglades at 2:00 am we went to their (my) lounge and entertained whoever they invited till 4:00 am We always had a bunch of different people and always had a good time!!!

Virginia Bradley Harold McVay and Harry Bradley

Mary and Harold McVay

Even when I went other places to work we would still end up there a lot of nights. Mary and Harold became really good friends and would come visit me everywhere I performed, Cincinnati, Akron, I never knew where they were going to show up and many times the Bradleys would come with them too.

The other people were Virginia and Harry Bradley, Dorothy Walker, and so many that became friends through the years…….

They became regular customers along with Virginia and Harry Bradley, Dorothy Walker, and Karl Jeney and wife, Joanne Farrell, who was a bartender at the Holiday Inn and who became the best friend I ever had.

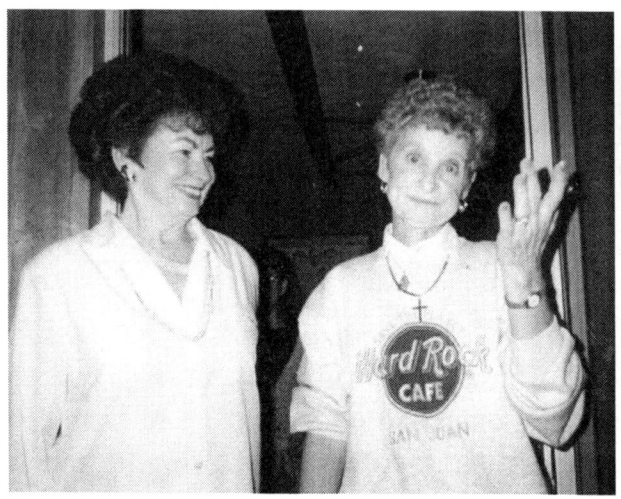

Me and Joanne   Harry and Virginia Bradley

In fact one afternoon Joanne invited me to stop by the Holiday Inn for a drink. When I got there all of my friends from the Everglades were there and so was the bartender (who was off that night). Well we all had a drink and then I told Joanne I had to leave because I had Mingo in the car and she said for me to bring him in. I sat him at the end of the bar on a barstool and he started to bark and bark and bark. Joanne came up and said what does that dog want, I told her a VO and water, she thought I was kidding but when she bought him one he took a sip and was very quiet the rest of the afternoon.

Needless to say that we all got to feeling pretty good and I told Joanne she had to come work with me tonight so she could sing in my place because I would probably be to "plowed," she promised she would be there then Tony called to tell the bartender that he had to work also and he was really "Plowed." Well to make a long story short……On my first set of the night I started off pretty good and then I got tickled and that was it. I confessed that I was slightly snookered and I was going to go down in the audience and party with everyone. I did just that and had a wonderful time with everyone that was there. Tony kept walking around and saying "My star, she is really drinking with everyone"!!! Tony had me driven back to my apartment after work and I woke up the next morning completely clothed with my purse and keys in my hand. It bought back memories of the time I was at the Boca.

I drove my little brother Bob out from Akron and he stayed with me for a week. Tony was so good to him, when he got tired he let him go sleep in his office until I got through work. He loved staying in the hotel and ordering room service!! He ran my bill up with all the goodies he ordered. At the supper club I would get him up and make him dance with me (twist). He had so much fun he didn't want to go home!

I had such a good time when I worked at the Everglades, they were a great audience and just lots of great people. I would drive to Akron on weekends to see my dad. I would leave at 2:00 in the morning on a Saturday night and would stay till Monday and come back in time to take Mingo to my apartment and go to work. I loved working the Everglades, my audience was almost always the same and the same people came in week after week.

One of the fun things that happened at the Everglades was when a song called *Funny Face* came out. I started getting requests for it and one night I went over and picked up a cute stuffed animal that a man in the audience had on his table and I sang Funny Face to it. Well that started a fun time because people started bringing me funny stuffed toys to sing *Funny Face* to. I would put them on the bandstand and at one point I had so many that it got to be really funny. Tony the owner finally came to me one day and said I had to take them down because people were asking him if they could buy them. So we cleared them off the stage.

Friends Forever

Joanne Farrell was my best friend for many years starting with the days I worked the Everglades in Columbus, Ohio. We were always good friends and I am still friends with her brother. When she found out she had cancer she had to undergo chemo and all the other things that went with it. Soon after that they found out that she had more cancer. She hated the chemo and all the other things she had to go through so she decided to not take any more chemo she expected to die right away when she stopped. She decided to sell her house and move into an apartment because her boyfriend said he did not want to live there after she died. She hated to sell it because she loved her home but decided that probably was best. After one year, she called me and said she had good news and bad news. I asked her what the good news was she said she was still alive but the bad news was that she was still living in that **** condo!.

We always called each other came to visit each other and then after about 4 years she called me and said she had Hospice but she wanted to have a drink with me in Las Vegas before she died. I told her I would fly to Ohio, she said no she wanted to have a drink with me in Las Vegas and that is what she did. I picked her up and the airport and for almost a week we had a great time together, the day before she was to go back she didn't feel too good. Her and her boyfriend, Jim went back home and she died soon after. It was a great loss to me she was my best friend and I still think of her often. Her brother, Dave is still a good friend to me, he has flown here to visit with his wife and he always sends me things on my computer. He is a great guy!

Joanne and Jim

Around Town
Conducted By
ROLAND SUNKER

Held over for the second time at the beautiful Desert Inn is the fabulous Miss De Lois and Her Music Men. Miss De Lois is no newcomer to the night people of Columbus. She has been one of the best, and also one of the favorite acts, to ever appear in Columbus. After many appearances Around Town, Lois' fans are always eager to welcome her back. This is because Lois is one of the best entertainers and a real trouper.

Without touching her act or changing one bit of material, Miss De Lois and Her Music Men were, in the past, simply great. It was hard to believe she could get better. But and there always has to be a "but," Lois has now taken over the stage in the Aztec Room with a brand new show, featuring a brand new drummer, Tiny Diamond. Both her show and her men, Tiny, and Jim on the organ, will stand up to any and all of the superlatives I might use.

To put it simply, Miss De Lois and Her Music Men have the greatest lounge act in the business.

Retaining some of the old numbers that have been Lois' trademarks and favorites of her fans, the show contains many new, up to date tunes. Not only has the material been improved, but the presentation is terrific. All new arrangements, with Jimmy and Tiny doing a lot of singing and also adding vocal support behind Lois, keeps the show moving at super speeds with tremendous pace and variety. Even her dance numbers have been revamped.

While in the show biz trade, Miss De Lois and Her Music Men are still considered a lounge act, I look at it as a "mini floor show." For those of you who have been to Las Vegas, it is a true Vegas type act. You take a look at it, and I think you will agree with this entire review. By the way, with Lois' figure and personality, you will want to look and look again, that's for sure.

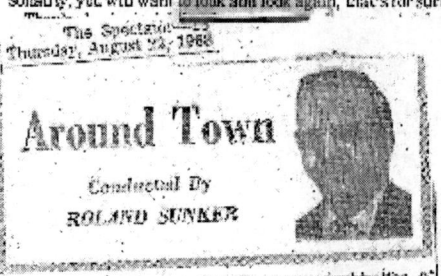

The Spectator—
Thursday, August 22, 1968

Around Town
Conducted By
ROLAND SUNKER

Personality plus, mixed with a rare combination of dancing and powerhouse song material, is the only way one can describe DeLois Phillips' Appearing nightly at the Everglades Restaurant. Miss DeLois and her Music Men have proved to be a great crowd pleaser.

Not since Les Paul and Mary Ford played the West Broad Street restaurant several years ago have there been such large audiences night after night.

DeLois incorporates songs and dances she has gathered from her appearances all over the world. In one evening she delights her audiences with Syrian, Hawaiian, Afro-Cuban and a tune she doesn't see in a night club any more, a good old fashioned tap dance.

Besides being talented, DeLoisian rates high for the beauty department. With her night grin, sparkling eyes and great personality, Miss DeLois is truly a stage rarity.

Wednesday, November 4, 1970
The Spectator

Miss De Lois & her Music Men return to Columbus!
Appearing in the Aztec Room
2 Weeks
NO COVER—NO MINIMUM
4 Shows Nightly
Music Begins at 9:30 P.M.
PHONE: 253-3436
DESERT INN
3840 E. Broad

Lois Phillips

Dancer-singer Lois Phillips is in the first week of her booking at the Rainbow Club after which she'll join the Charlie Spivak orchestra in Haven, Fla., for a month, then on to be featured with Guy Lombardo at his Port O'Call resort, near St. Pete-Tampa, Fla.

LOIS PHILLIPS

Lois Phillips has delighted audiences in Detroit, Cleveland and Canada with her dancing, singing and exciting personality. You'll be delighted too.

3 SHOWS NIGHTLY
9:30 — 11:30 — 1 A.M.

The finest Italian and American Cuisine being served every night at the Bella Vista

Bella Vista 
Atop the Rims
AL 2-1581

WYOMING PEOPLE—Be sure to tune your dial to KOOK Radio at 11:30 Friday nite for our show direct from the Bella Vista.

Around Town

Conducted By ROLAND SUNKER

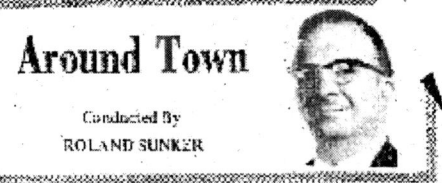

One of the most entertaining and refreshing acts in show biz is currently in the El Black Rose Lounge of the Imperial House-North.

Miss DeLois and her Music Men are no strangers to the night people of Columbus. But she and her men are always as welcome back to Columbus as the first day of spring. There are many reasons why Miss DeLois is as refreshing and delightful as a spring day.

First, she is the personification of showmanship. This little red-haired girl is a real trouper on stage. Lois knows just about every trick in the trade when it comes to selling her talents. On or off stage, she is a warm, personable individual. These traits alone, are enjoyable for her audience.

Her material is also quite entertaining. Most of it is in the novelty, comedy and special material category. The songs of Miss DeLois are not the same, old, worn-out tunes you hear everywhere you go. They are Lois and fun. And, of course, she can put them across. Besides singing, Lois is an accomplished dancer, with routines ranging from the intriguing Oriental moods, to the exotic Hawaiian gals and, for good measure, the good, old-fashioned rousing tap which is always a crowd pleaser.

Add all of this together, along with two very fine musicians, organist Jimmy Melis and drummer John Maruiott, and you come out with a high-powered, explosive act. Lois paces her act well, and keeps the whole thing moving as if she was running from a carload of TNT. At times you get the feeling that she was of about met head on, resulting in a giant, bombastic evening of entertainment.

If Miss DeLois and Her Music Men can't entertain you, regardless of age or gender, then I think you are beyond all hope. Make sure you catch her soon at the Imperial House-North. When it comes to making you forget your problems and troubles of the day, she has a magic wand, called show business, to accomplish this feat.

El "Black Rose" RESTAURANT and COCKTAIL LOUNGE

MISS DeLOIS and her Music Men

Female Vocalist and Exotic Dancer

3 shows nightly
9—10:30—12

Every Tuesday Ladies' Nite
All Drinks ½ Price

AT IMPERIAL HOUSE MOTEL • I-75 & BY-PASS 50
CINCINNATI, OHIO 45227 • PHONE 771-0870

6—Metro

Lincoln Lodge Offers A Rare Talent—DeLois

This is one of those times when as a person and reviewer I wish I'd gotten there sooner. Where? Lincoln Lodge. Why? A very special form of entertainment has been taking place for the past four weeks. Her name is DeLois and she's tops as female entertainers who can really make music are rare.

The act closes Saturday evening so between now and then, stop by the cocktail lounge and see what DeLois has that is rare.

It is one and many various talents, personality and stage presence that are playing to a full capacity audience. Impish grin, sparkling eyes, a rich voice, accomplished dancing and a natural performer make DeLois a rarity.

Starting her career professionally some six years back she started as a dancer and was under contract to Charlie Spivac for four years. She graduated from high school at the age of 16 and has had two years at Kent State University.

Much of DeLois' repertoire is based on "torch songs" but how can one with such a girlish grin be sultry? She manages and with distinction.

Uncommon in Columbus' night spots is a traveling microphone. She uses one, to her delight and that of the audiences. This rendition of something out of the past certainly adds to the air of comfort at Lincoln Lodge.

She'll charm you with her interpretation of an about-to-be-married Greek girl's dance. There is no comparison, thanks to her delivery through class and style.

This is her first appearance in Columbus, but with her personality and talent she'll be around for awhile.

FRI. NOV. 19, 1971

DeLois Phillips and Her Music Men

Costuming from both hemispheres, songs from the deep south to New York's west side, a touch of Syrian belly dancing, stroboscopic and ultraviolet lighting effects...

No, it's not an extravaganza (at least in size), it's the personable, fast-moving act of Miss DeLois and Her Men, performing nightly through Saturday at Lincoln Lodge.

(If you catch her not moving report to the management — it's probably a breach of contract). She has one of the most pleasant, controlled and versatile voices on the night scene.

The "Down Home" flavor of her origins comes through only on country and western numbers such as "I Didn't Promise You A Rose Garden" or "A Little Bitty Tear."

NIGHTLY IN THE COCKTAIL LOUNGE

LINCOLN LODGE

1850 W. BROAD ST.   878-5341

COLUMBUS SPOTLIGHT
OCT. 18 - 31

Your complete guide to Columbus...
DINING, EVENTS, ENTERTAINMENT

MISS ALBERGHETTI
ANDY LAUNER
LINDA RONSTADT
MISS DeLOIS

HEADLINERS:

GLORIA LORING
ALLAN JONES
COLUMBUS SYMPHONY
EUGENE ISTOMIN

Family Matters

Then after a year of working at the Everglades, Mom called to let me know my dad died. I was heartbroken and I went to Akron immediately. I stayed with Mom and Bob a few days after the funeral and then I had to go back to work. My first night back I walked out on the stage and all the lights went out and everyone lit a candle. In those days that was always done when someone lost someone. It was done to show the person who lost a love one that everyone was in their corner and cared. It was hard to entertain that night…………..

I felt so sorry for Mom and my brothers. Ron had joined the service. He was gone but I kept going back and forth from Columbus for quite a while. I decided I needed to help my mom and I looked for a job around Akron.

I did work one and that was not pleasant, they wanted me to stay after my first two weeks and I told the guy that owned it I couldn't because I had other places I was booked. My closing night my brother Ron had come home to visit and he came to help me get Jim's organ out and while he was on the stand the owner pulled a gun and said he could not take it out. That he was not going to let me leave. I jumped in front of the gun because it was pointed at my brother Ron and I pointed it away from him and my brother ran to me and said we should leave. So I left and I called the union the next day and they said they would take care of the problem….within minutes I got a call from the owner telling me I could pick up the organ so Ron went with me and we got it, the owner even helped us get it out. The next day Jim and I were on our way to our next "gig."

Between the union in Detroit and several other friends I was always helped out of some difficult situations. Anyway I finally decided to stay around Ohio and I bought a house. Mom sold her house and moved to Columbus and I let mom live in the top part of my new house. It had a beautiful basement that was built into a big room with a fireplace, a big bedroom, a bar and a place you could go upstairs to a patio, so that is where I lived. Then I decided to buy a cocktail lounge of my own. I found out there was one in Gahanna and I bought it.

Well, being an entertainer most of my life I really didn't know all the ins and outs of running a cocktail lounge. I found out after I bought it that they had kind of a tough crowd which stupidly I did not know. Anyway when I opened it was a learning experience and I sent postcards to all of my former "followers" and they all showed up opening night. It was wonderful except for halfway thorough we had a bunch of really rough guys come in and when I saw them I told the guys in my band that we would just play all the beautiful songs and waltzes, well it worked, the lead guy got up and said to me "You're a hot broad but I don't like your music so we are leaving!!! I was thrilled and on the next set we did all of our show things and we packed the place!!

Owning a bar was an experience I won't forget. I let mom tend bar during the daytime which was one of the biggest mistakes I made. A gang of young guys came in and she became sort of a "mother figure" to them and they were from time to time getting free drinks. It took me awhile to straighten that out but I did get the job done!!

It was also difficult for me; I drank in a bar before but never owned one. Ordering booze I left up to the bartender and checking out every night after performing all night was not fun and a little scary. Some friends of mine who I had worked for came in one night and told me I should have told them I wanted a bar I could have "fronted" one of theirs and not spent my own money. While they were there they taught me a lot. They wanted me to watch my bartender and I saw how he was ringing up one drink and pocketing the next one they showed me all the ways he was stealing from me and even though I felt very naive I was mad and I went back behind the bar and even though we were crowded I fired him on the spot. He said to me you can't fire me you have a full house and I told him I did fire him. I had one of the guys in my band string the mike behind the bar and for the rest of the night I sang and mixed drinks.

It was great talking to all the people and singing to them as I mixed their drinks. I had a great time and made more money that night then I had ever made since I owned it. My friends that helped me got a big kick out of what I did and they slipped me $200 because they never saw anything like that before. I really appreciated what they showed me because the next bartender I hired I knew what to look for and I really knew what I was doing.

I realized a lot of things after the bartender I fired left, things like the bottles of "Jim Beam" was hardly used (that was my bartender's favorite drink!). Then, the guy I bought the bar from called me into his office one day, I found out that most of the people that had bought the bar after a few months had to give it back to the owner because they couldn't make a go of it so he just took it back and had done that for several years. I was a little suspicious when he did call me so when I went I took my checkbook. He looked at me when I came in and said I know you are probably not making any money and not doing well so I will take the bar back if it would help you……..I smiled and said no, I love the bar but I'm glad you called this meeting because I wanted to pay you off, so I did. I thought he was going to faint!!! It was great experience. I was doing well and I did have good times, but it was a lot of responsibility you don't have when you are just an entertainer.

I owned Miss DeLois Lounge for a few years. After the first year I was there I decided to look for a house in Gahanna. I found one with a pool in the backyard and a bar. It needed a lot of work but it was closer to my bar and I got it for a really good price. I had the pool redone and filled and I had all of my friends that I met at the Everglades over for parties. Even Joe Lavinger came over and played in my pool. It was always a good time when friends came.

74

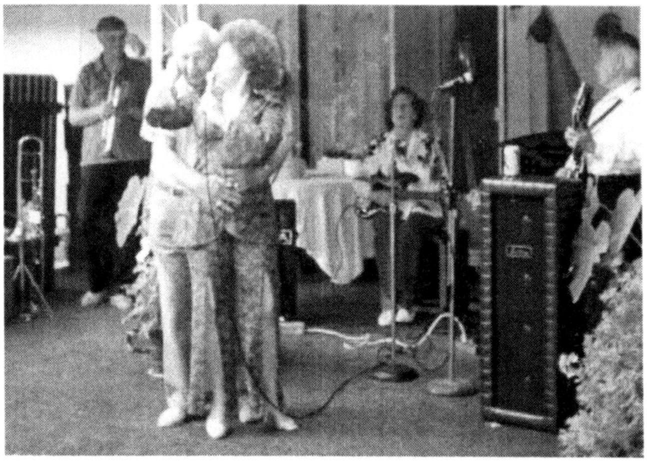

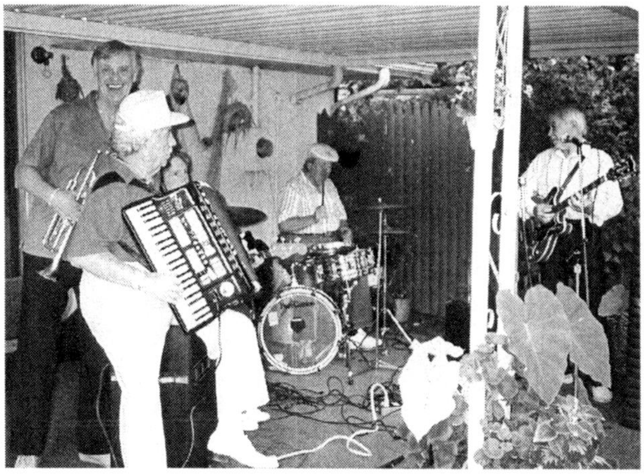

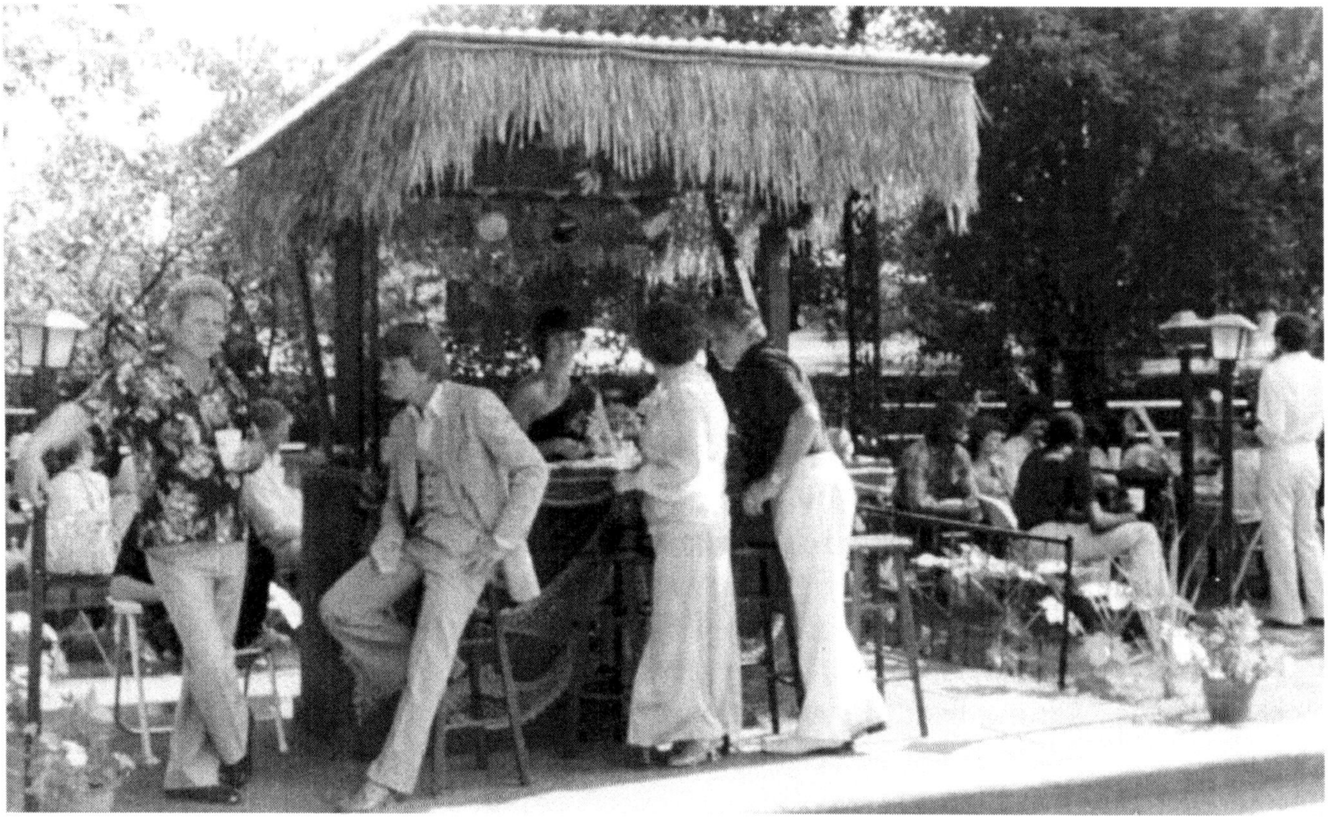

❧ Marriage

Shortly after that I met my first husband. He was about my age, blond hair, blue eyes and really sweet to me when I met him. I had always felt uneasy checking out at night at the bar by myself and going out to my car alone. Because he was so tough and seemed so protective of me, he made me feel safe when he stayed with me while I checked out at night. I thought he was a nice guy and he treated me very well. He said he had been married and had two children. We started out just spending time together and to make a long story short I was so naive that when he asked me to marry him I said yes.

I started planning my marriage and I told all of my friends. I got a call from Jack LaDelle, he said he and his mother were in town and he needed to talk to me. I met him and he asked me not to get married. Well, I thought he was just jealous; and I told him no. I had already planned my wedding and I thought I loved my husband to be. He was so upset, and when I left him, I really felt bad. I had always loved Jack but my ex was younger and stronger and then I was really in turmoil. But when I saw him that evening I just forgot all my feelings that I had earlier.

We planned our wedding in a church and my family, except for my brother Ron, who was in secret service, were all there. My brother Bob gave me away. Before the wedding I told my bridesmaids that I thought I was making a mistake and I decided that I wasn't going to marry him. They said I was just nervous like most brides and for me to calm down and get ready to walk down the aisle, I told them I would rather run out the back door but I went through with it.

I knew in my heart I had made a mistake, I still had feelings for Jack. But that night we went to my bar for our after wedding party and the place was loaded with all my friends, I was still in my gown and got up and sang with my band. I even sat on the end of the stage and took off my garter and threw it out to the audience.

76

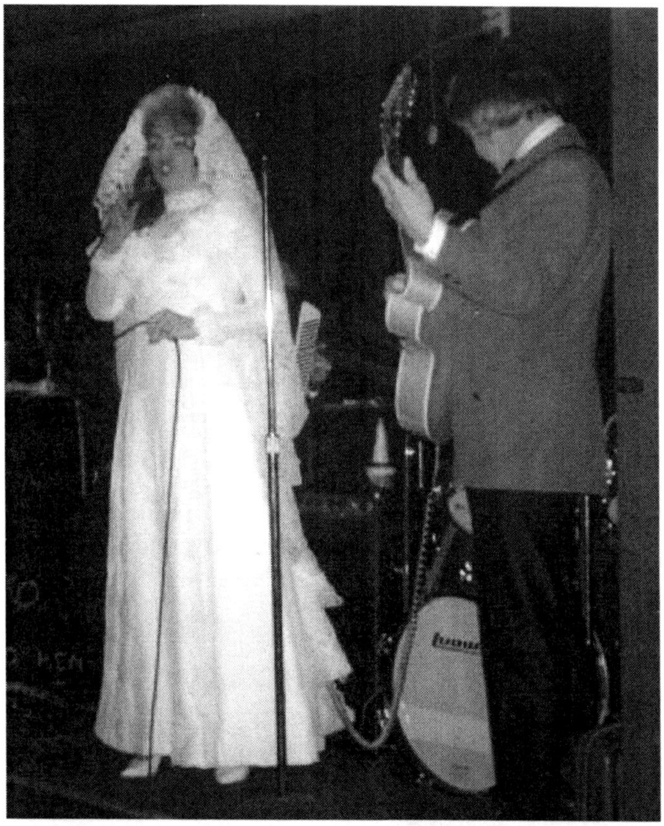

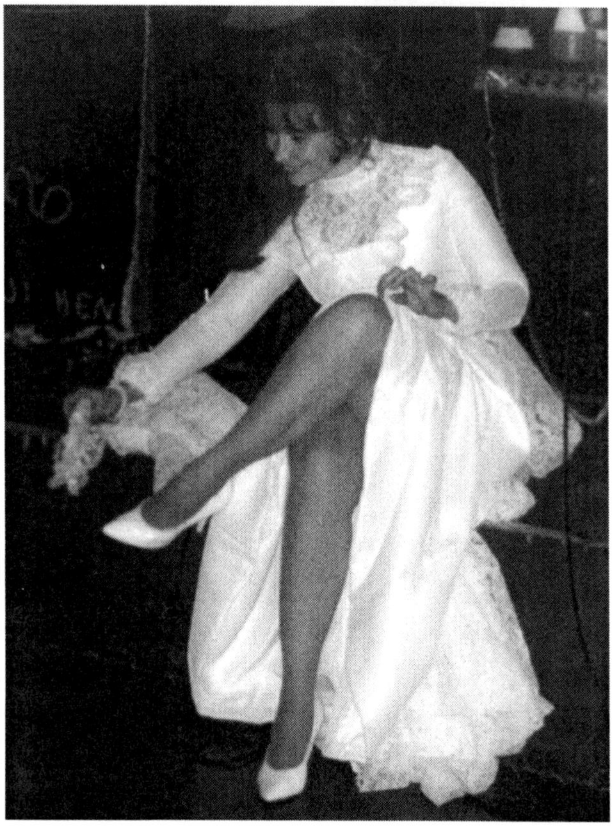

Then later on I changed clothes and Mom and my new husband got up on the stand and talked to everyone and called me up to join them. He told everyone they got a drink on the house and we were going to join them and celebrate! And that is what we did!!!

Later on that night I felt like I had made the biggest mistake of my life! If I could erase anything about my life it would have been my marriage to him. It was also then that I found out that he had four kids instead of two.

It changed my whole life. I kept working as an entertainer using my real name DeLois and using my husband's last name. He was so jealous, first of the bus boy at the hotel, and then he was jealous of my mother, my brother, Bob and anyone who looked at me including my dog!!!! I tried really hard to make it work. One afternoon I told him I was going to meet my brother Bob for a drink. I drove to a little bar down the street and I found Bob and we were sitting there when my husband came in and looked all around the bar and when he found us he said I just didn't believe you met your brother here!! There was even a time when one of his friends was in town and wanted us to go on a vacation with him and he wanted us to take my mom with us. We did and later after that was over and we were home my husband accused me of having an affair with his friend, I had to laugh to myself because it was my mother who had the affair with him, not me. But at this point I didn't even waste my breath to tell him!

I tried for several years to make a go of my marriage. He would take off to Florida taking two of his kids and me and all I did there was cook and take care of everyone. He also never got a job and was running up all of my credit cards. We were living in the house I had bought in Gahanna and it just got worse and worse.

Shortly after that, my little Mingo was crossing the street one night with my mother's German shepherd and right before he got to the curb he got hit by a car. He was almost on the curb and this man swerved his car towards him and hit him. I was so mad, I picked up Mingo and cried and took him to the vet, and I couldn't believe he was dead. I hated losing him; he had been through so much with me and he was such a good dog.

It was shortly after that Joanne gave me a Lhasa apso, which I named Sinbad and another friend gave me a Cairn terrier which I called Max.

Because I was from the "old school," I really tried to make my marriage work so I quit entertaining and took a day time job in an office. I went from making $1,000 a week to $4.50 an hour. I got a job as a receptionist at Ohio Laborers. I liked my job and I found out that the things I had learned in my father's office when I was a kid all came back to me. I didn't tell anyone I had been an entertainer in the office I just said I was married and needed to get a job.

My Brother Ron

Not long after that Ron met a lady by the name of Judy who was a nurse; and he really fell head over heels in love with her. He married her shortly after that.

Judy was not happy that Ron was in the Secret Service and after a few years she made him quit. Ron was really in love with Judy and did everything he could to please her. When he quit Secret Service he moved them back to the states and bought a big piece of property in Perris (now Riverside) California. He got a job at Merrill Lynch and worked there for a few years. Then Judy had him quit and talked him into opening a feed store and also raising Morgan horses on their ranch. He put in a track, built stables and everything was great.

Ron was always good at building things. He made them a beautiful place with a great patio in the middle of his beautiful trees to just sit and relax. He brought his dog with him that he had oversees; and it was so sad when he got attacked by coyotes and was killed. I felt so sorry for Ron, he was heartbroken.

When I had a chance I would go down to visit Ron and Judy on a weekend. One of the times when I was there Ron left early before I got up to go down to the feed store and when I got up Judy told me she was going to work. So after she left I decided to get into Ron's big truck and drive it down to see him if I could find his keys. He was so surprised when I got down there that I was driving his big four on the floor truck. I admit it took me a few minutes to get used to it but I made it. Ron was so tickled. We always had some laughs when we were together! He loved to tease me! When I got upset about something he would pick me up and put me on the refrigerator!

I enjoyed my new job and after a few months the boss's secretary decided to leave and she suggested that I interview for her possession. I didn't think I had a chance to get it but I did. The boss was wonderful to work for and I really enjoyed it, but when I went home to tell my husband that I got the job he said to me what did you do, go to bed with him…. Needless to say that really hurt my feelings.

I was so happy Ron was living back in the states. I finally decided I could not live the rest of my life like I was living it so instead of going to Florida with my husband and his kids I flew out to visit Ron. When he picked me up at the airport I cried all the way to his house. He fixed me a Manhattan and I told him my whole story. I told him I had decided to get a divorce when I got back, I just couldn't live the rest of my life like this.

I had a wonderful week with him and his wife Judy and I discovered that I don't think I ever really loved my husband, that I should have listened to my first instinct and left on my wedding day. Ron and Judy were very supportive of me and when I flew back to Ohio I told my husband I wanted a divorce. He fixed himself a drink and told me no, then after a few more drinks he agreed to give me a divorce and he would let me keep the house (which was mine to begin with) if I paid off his credit cards. So I agreed to do that.

The day we got our divorce he stood up and court and said to me you may be divorced but I'm not and if someone touches a hair on your head I will kill them. That was scary and not at all fun to live with! Well I thought I would go back into show business, however on the day of our divorce he told everyone that if I decided to go back in the business he would beat up the person I was working for. I did not think he would do something like that.

I called all of my creditors and asked them if I could just pay them a little at a time, I explained my situation and they all worked with me. A few days later my best friend Joanne called and said I should go out to dinner with her to cheer me up. We went to the Everglades where I had worked and left my car there so we could go to another restaurant we liked and we were going to come back there and listen to the music. When we got through with dinner we went back to the Everglades.

We went into the bar for a drink and some politicians that used to see me perform came over and I started talking to them, they all asked what happened and I began to cry as I told them my whole story. One of them said he would get me an interview at the Public Utilities Commission because I could make more money there and I was thrilled. He said he couldn't guarantee anything but it would be worth a try because they were looking for a secretary. I was thrilled and I told him I would call the next day and ask for an interview. I went out to get in my car and it wouldn't start. I had to call AAA and they came out and looked at it, someone had torn the whole insides out, so Joanne gave me a ride home. When I got home my ex called me, he thought I was out with someone else because my car was there and I wasn't. He said he would do it again if he caught me with someone. I was so afraid of him.

The next day I called the Public Utilities Commission and I got an interview for a secretary for the Public Interest Center. I had my interview with Marsha Ryan. She was very thorough and asked me many questions. She said she would get back to me in the next week but she told me she thought I had a good chance of landing the job. I was praying that I would get that job because it would give me a chance to pay off my credit cards that my ex-husband ran up. I was so thrilled two days later when I received a call that I got the job. I started that next Monday. I loved my boss at Ohio Laborers but when I explained my situation to him he was very understanding. He told me he was sad to see me go but he understood my reason.

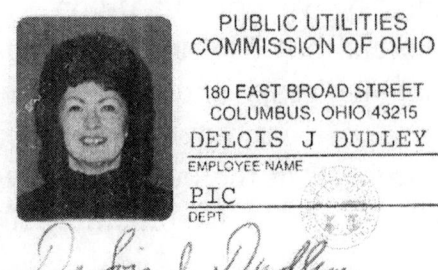

I was so nervous my first day on my new job and when I got there they fired my boss. Well then I was really nervous. But everyone was so helpful and showed me around and told me that my new boss would be starting in a week. I wanted to make a good impression so I really talked to everyone and found out what my duties would be and started working immediately.

A New Beginning

I stayed working at the Public Utilities Commission and I did shows on weekends. I got all of my bills caught up and kept my house. I kept getting promoted at the Public Interest Center and I ended up being an administrative assistant. I had several different bosses through the years and I trained and liked all of them.

I worked for a while with Marsha Ryan, the lady who hired me. Then one day my new boss came in, Lisa Kirk. She was wonderful and I got along with her very well. I really enjoyed the Public Utilities and I became friends with the attorney there, Charlie, and he was a great guy; he was very good to me. To this day we are still friends and he calls me quite often.

Then while I was working in Columbus I got a call from Ron. Judy had left him for a priest. While he was working she divided everything in the house and even half of the horses and left him a note. My heart broke for him. I told him I would take off from work and get a plane and fly there as soon as I could. I called Jan Maiden and told her I had an emergency and I had to take off a few days to go see my brother in California. I got a flight out the next day. Ron was happy to see me when I arrived although I could tell his heart was breaking. I made us a drink and we went outside on his patio.

It is the first and only time I have ever seen Ron sob. I felt so sorry for him. I couldn't believe that Judy could do such a thing to him. He had a little picture in his kitchen that said "we will be together forever." I hugged him and we talked for long time and I fixed him dinner. My heart broke seeing him like that. I spent several days with him and hated to leave but I needed to go back to work. I couldn't believe it but shortly after that Judy called and asked me if we could remain friends. I told her that if she had told Ronnie she didn't love him and was honest with him things might be different but for her to walk out like a thief

83

in the middle of his work hours and take half of everything even the horses and the dishes I told her I didn't want to see or speak to her again!!! Every time she called after that I just hung up on her! Ron dated several girls after that and was with one for quite awhile but basically didn't seem that interested in any of them. Ron has always been special to me and we have always been there for each other whenever we needed to be.

When I got back to work everyone was happy to see me and the very next day I received a call from my ex-husband. He told me that he had met a lady and she wanted him to go to Florida (his favorite place) with her and buy a trailer. He said he was still in love with me but I told him that I was never good enough for him and he should go with her. I have to admit I had my fingers crossed every moment of our conversation. When he told me he was going to leave with her I was so happy I cried. That night I went out and celebrated with my friend Joanne. From that day my whole life changed.

The next few years were wonderful, my work was good, my life was good and everything for me was great! I did shows around town, worked with Joe Lavinger and his band on weekends and continued my day time job during the week. Then I went out to visit my brother Ronnie for his birthday. While I was there he decided to take me to Vegas and we would celebrate his birthday there. I loved to play craps and in the old days it was my favorite game and sometimes the guys at the table when I was working there would give me the sign and I could shill for them.

I just loved to play not for the money but for the excitement. I told my brother that I would take $50.00 to the crap table and whatever I made we would spend celebrating his birthday. Well, I was there about an hour and I ended up collecting about $500.00.

Needless to say I was so happy and when we left the table to go to the bar I was so surprised when I sat down to look at the other side of the bar and see Jack LaDelle. Ron asked him if he wanted to join us and he accepted and we all had a good time and I felt the spark I always had for Jack light up again inside me. I told Jack that I was no longer married and that I was working in Ohio at the Public Utilities Commission. He asked me if I would mind if he would call me from time to time and of course I said no, I wouldn't mind at all.

Many years later I found out that Ronnie and he had planned that accidental meeting. I went back to Ronnie's and spent the rest of the week with him and I even got a couple of calls from Jack there. I went back to Ohio thinking about Jack on the plane. I think I realized that I really had always loved him…….. When I got back to work I was busy again.

I loved my job at the PUCO and also loved doing the shows on weekends at different places. Jack began calling me more often and then decided to fly out to see me. I was really happy. I bought him back from the airport to my home and he really thought it was nice and we sat outside and had a drink and went in the pool. It was fun being back with him. He loved his Martinis and of course I had those with him. I introduced him to my friends, the McKay's, Bradley's and everyone else I could think of. We had a great time and then it was time for him to go back home to Vegas. I really missed him and I realized more and more that I was still in love with him.

But I went back to my regular routine and we talked almost every other day. I had little Sinbad and he was always so much good company. I had lost my little Terrier about a year before so Sinbad was all I had. Jack showed me a picture of his dog when he was visiting me. He had a dog that was a white German shepherd and wolf. Jack called him Foxy. Jack told me he kept him outside his house in his fenced in yard. I kept on working and doing my shows on weekends at the Lincoln Lodge. I worked there for a long time and always enjoyed it.

I did really miss Jack and it wasn't long after he visited that he sent me a ticket to go visit him and I went. We had a good time and went to several places, I got to see where he was living and I really loved being with him. Before I left there Jack said to me that I had always said I wanted a place to live in Vegas that was far enough from the strip to lead a normal life but close enough to still have all the things I loved so he bought two and a half acres of land and he asked me to marry him. I told him that I loved him and was so glad he bought the land but I just had so much things in Ohio that I would just have to think about it ………..

I got on the plane and all the way home all I could think of was that I really had always loved him and how stupid I was to not marry him, when I got off the plane I went directly to the phone at the airport and called him and told him I would marry him. He said "good, go get my ticket that he had ordered for me at the ticket counter and fly back." I laughed, that was how well he really knew me so I went and got my ticket and flew back. He had my brother Ron there and we went to a justice of peace and got married right away! I had to go back to Ohio because I had work, a house, a dog and thousands of other things. We talked

86

and I knew it would take me some time to get things settled but I was so happy to be Mrs. Jack LaDelle Stallcup!!! (After all these years)

❧ Las Vegas

I surprised everyone when I came back to Ohio and told them I had married Jack. I knew it would take some time to figure out all the things I had to take care of, my job, my house, etc. Almost every other day Jack would call me and tell me what he was doing and when he was going to start to build a house on the land. I was so thrilled. I was still trying to figure out all the things I needed to do and after several months Jack sent me a ticket and I went back out. I got to see the house and the land and I really fell in love with it.

There was nothing around it that was close; it was near Blue Diamond and there was only one house near us and that was not in walking distance. We even spent my first night in it with no furniture but we built a fire in the fire place and bought food and our martinis there and had a wonderful time. Ron called me the next day and said how happy he was that I would eventually be closer to him.

I had a hard time leaving there. I loved the way it felt to be there. I knew it was the place I really should be. The skies were beautiful at night and in the day and it was so gorgeous where we were I really loved it. All my life I had always thanked the Lord for what I had and it was there that I felt so much closer to Him. All the way back to Ohio I was making plans to come back and live the rest of my life in a place that I really loved with a man that I really loved. I told my mother, my brother Bob and all my friends and my boss Lisa about my leaving.

I decided to let my mother stay in my house and Bob was going to stay there in the bottom of it. It took a lot longer for me to get ready to leave than I thought. I wanted to help Lisa, and I tried to take care of everything that I needed to take care of. I went through all the things she needed to know the next day and worked with her and protected her from lots of the things that went on there. I am proud to say she is still there. Lisa was and still is a very pretty lady and is a good friend even today.

Jack and Ronnie came out to Ohio and we rented a truck and took all the things I wanted to take to Vegas, even my flowers and packed them up. We had a great time going back and I was so excited. I decided to just retire from show business although I had some shows I had to do that I had already signed up for (my husband Jack said that he knew me well enough to know that I would never stop entertaining for good, he used to tell people he had the only wife in the world who when she opened the refrigerator sang two courses before she closed it) but I was sure that that was what I was going to do. Ron and Jack unloaded the truck and I was so happy with the house. The yard was huge, we had 2 ½ acres.

Anyway my life began very nicely in Las Vegas. When Ron left and went back to California Jack and I fixed a nice fire in the fireplace and we had our martinis with my little Sinbad. He was getting close to 14, but he still liked his booze and chocolate. Jack could say cocktail time and he would be the first in line. I wasn't sure at first that Jack and Sinbad would get along but they really hit it off. Jack would take him for a walk around out big back yard and he used to come in and say your two old men took a walk around the yard. I gave them both a hug!

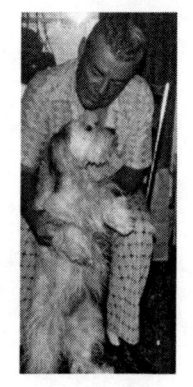

I decided I was just going to get my outside organized and plant some things in the front and back yard. I laughed at my former boss Lisa who was calling me and saying that she wanted me to come back she didn't know she had the "problem" people that she had. I laughed and told her that that was my job to keep them from her. She couldn't believe all the things that were happening when I wasn't there. So every few days I was getting calls from the PUCO and Jack joked with me saying that he thought I was still working there!!!!!!!

I started planting some roses in the back; I planted some evergreens out front and some tall evergreens around the front gate and some other plants all around different places in the yard. My brother Ron bought me 14 roses for my birthday and I planted them in the front of my house. I went back into the back and we decided to put grass in the back and I planted some little palm trees. I went down to Plantworld and the gentlemen there gave me several palms that he said he didn't think would make it but because they weren't doing too well, he gave me a special price. Well I love palms so I said yes and went home and tried to plant them around the back of my yard in case they didn't make it. They grow very slow but they are all still alive today!

While I was planting all of a sudden a cute little squirrel appeared. I ran into the house and got some nuts and I started feeding them to him. He would follow me around the yard and examine everything I planted. Then one night I introduced him to Jack. We were having our martinis outside on the patio and the little squirrel appeared and jumped up in my lap, I gave him a nut and he jumped down and sat next to us and ate his nuts. Sinbad just ignored him; he was busy having his evening drink! We got a big kick out of the squirrel and for some reason I named him Herman!

Herman got into a habit every night at cocktail hour he would come and pound on our glass door. I would let him in and he ate nuts while we all had our drinks. This went on for about two months, then one night Herman came in had his nuts and decided to not leave. He hid and we had a terrible time trying to find him. My husband had his office upstairs. We had a nice upstairs with a bar, kitchen, bathroom and a large room that had our desks and a long sofa in it. The next morning my husband was upstairs at his desk and I got a call from him telling me to close the door downstairs because the squirrel was upstairs. We tried for several weeks to catch him but with no luck.

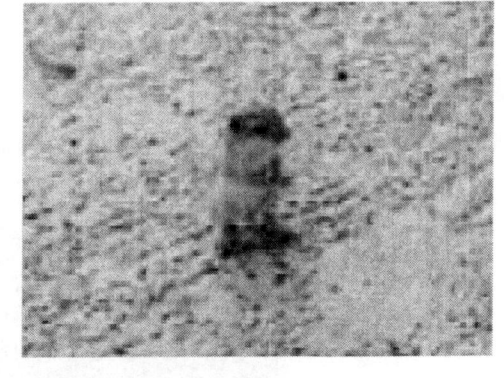

Finally my husband rigged up a flat piece of wood that he put on the ground and a cover that went over it. He hooked the cover to a string and he put all kinds of squirrel treats on the flat piece starting from the outside to the center. He then put the cover over the flat piece and pulled the string clear over to his desk and held it in his hand while he read. Herman came out of his hiding place and went over to the piece in the floor and took one of the nuts that was close to the end of the cover and ran, my husband just sat there and held the string in his hand, several minutes later the squirrel came out again and grabbed another nut, he kept doing that until he got into the center of the flat piece and my husband dropped the top and it captured the squirrel underneath, my husband was so happy and called me to come upstairs and we opened the door and went out to the outside patio we had upstairs and he lifted the top and the squirrel ran down the stairs to the outside patio and out in the back yard!. My husband was so proud of himself and we really laughed about the whole ordeal.

The next morning however as I was fixing breakfast I heard something scratching on my patio door and there was Herman trying to get back in! We had so much fun with that. The next few months were just fun enjoying my house, my husband and my little Sinbad.

Jack had Foxy still in town in his other house because he was afraid he would hurt Sinbad. I had about ten contracts for shows I had to honor so I was flying out periodically with Sinbad to do them. I finished my commitments and finished all of my shows and told Jack I was going to get a day time job and retire from show business, he just laughed. He asked me if I ever thought about teaching dancing. I told him I didn't want to teach amateurs that I didn't mind teaching pros but I didn't think I would like teaching people that had never danced before. With that he kind of smiled and changed the subject. I did tell him that I decided to just get a daytime job because after I fixed up my house I would be bored.

The next day I put my applications in several places in town and got a call from AHEC. I went in to interview and did not mention my show business life but told her about my Public Utilities Commission job and the other jobs I had worked in Ohio, about two days later I got a call and they hired me! It was an interesting job and I enjoyed my boss at that time. I worked and came home and my husband and I enjoyed our cocktail hours and always had a good dinner and life was good. Little Sinbad was doing well and he cared about Jack and they got along good. I was still working "gigs on the weekends and was still having fun! I worked for AHEC quite awhile and enjoyed it.

AHEC decided to move their office into UMC and it was really different for me. My boss decided to leave and one of the girls in the office by the name of Rose Yuhos took over her position. I held down my place and while I was there I got to know a lot of the people at UMC. All the doctors and the people that worked there were all nice to me and I enjoyed it. Then one afternoon I was told by one of my friends there that I should apply for an opening with one of the doctors. His name was Dr. Kaiser. I had seen him and spoke with him once in a while but really did not know him. I thought that would be nice and the money they were offering was considerably better than what I was getting so I applied. I found him very pleasant and when he offered me the job I was really surprised and excited. The next day I gave my two week notice to AHEC.

Working for Dr. Kaiser was a new experience and I found him very nice and easy to work for. At the time he was the head of the smoking censation program. I also got to meet and work with Dr. Susan Steinberg who was a very nice lady. She was very nice to me and we worked well together.

Shortly after starting work for Dr. Kaiser I met a lady by the name of Marion Gibson who lived close to me. We started having lunch and going shopping and we became friends. I had not told anyone that I met when I came here that I had been an entertainer nor that I knew anything about dancing. She was taking tap from a lady called Peggy Ryan, and asked me if I would like to go to one of her lessons. I told her that I would go and I went the next day to her class. I tried to act like I didn't know anything about tapping and I got into the back line. I got to meet a lot of ladies there and they were all just having fun. After being there a couple of weeks the teacher moved me up into the front line....it was hard to act like I had never danced and sometimes I would forget and I think she noticed that. It was kind of boring for me but I did get to meet a lot of nice ladies, some that I am still friends with today.

We had our first Christmas and Bob and my mother came out to our house and Ronnie and his girlfriend as well. It was a great Christmas. We had a real fire in the fireplace and we had a wonderful few days together.

Jack and I had a wonderful time in our new home and I worked hard trying to get it organized. I finally got everything in place and Jack and I were enjoying our life together. I was still doing shows occasionally and going with Marion to tap dance class.

My mother started calling me more often. She said she was unhappy and I felt sorry for her. I talked to Ron and we decided to go out there on Mother's day.

When we got there she was so surprised to see us. We were there a short time when Bob came home, he was surprised to see me and I fixed him a drink and said we were all having dinner together.

92

After that night I decided that perhaps I should make arrangements to come back and take Mom back with me and put my house up for sale. I told Mom and Bob that was what I planned to do. So Ron and I flew back and made plans to get a truck and drive back to pick up Mom and her belongings and put my house up for sale. When I got back I told Jack what I was going to do and although he was not thrilled he did not complain. He was never really thrilled with my mother starting from the time we were all in my basement in Ohio and my mother called down the stairs and said we had to leave right away because Bob had to go to work the next morning and she loved him more than she ever loved Ron and me. Because all my friends were there I really felt hurt but Jack turned around at the bar and told my mother, Bonnie if you need to take Bob home get a cab, we are going to stay longer! From that day forward Jack was not thrilled with my mother!! The next day I called an agent I knew in Ohio and listed my house. I figured Bob would be able to find him an apartment. I asked Ron if he would go with me back to Ohio and he said yes. Ron was always someone I could count on my whole life.

We got back to Ohio and loaded up all of Mom's belongings and cleaned up the house and started back to Vegas. After driving about an hour Mom started acting like she didn't know either one of us. We tried talking to her but she did not realize who we were. It was a bit heartbreaking and scary. I tried to calm her down but she kept talking to Ron more than me and didn't seem to know what she wanted to do. Needless to say our ride home was not a good one. I told Ron I thought I needed to take her to a doctor. When we got her home she seemed to get her memory back but it wasn't long after that she started acting funny again and I decided I needed to take her to a doctor.

When I took her a week later they ran some tests and I found out mom had Alzheimer's. I didn't know much about that and I looked it up on my computer and tried to learn as much as I could. I decided to dance one more time for her while she knew who I was and I started practicing at Henry LaTang's studio. He and his wife were so tickled. When I told them I was going to enter in a contest so my mom could see me dance Henry said he was just happy I was going to dance again and that he was sure I would win. Shortly after that I was rehearsing at his studio and his wife came in to tell me not to leave but to go into Henry's class to see him. So I did. I sat down and a few minutes after I came in the door opened and there stood Gregory Hines. He was a student of Henry's and Henry was so glad to see him they gave each other a big hug and he said to Henry let me see your students dance. They all got up and did their number. Then Gregory pointed at me and said let me see you dance. Henry went to the piano and started playing and I got up to dance and then Gregory joined me and we did challenges. It was great fun and when we stopped he called me the lady with the fancy feet. I thanked him so much and told him how much fun I had!! He was very nice to me.

I went on with my practicing and the day of the competition I took Mom with me and put her in the audience with a friend and went back to get ready to perform. To make a long story short, I won 1st place and when they announced it to the audience I did not know that Gregory and Henry were in the audience and Gregory went up to the judges and asked if he could give me my trophy. They were all surprised and said yes, so to my surprise he came out on the stage and handed me the trophy and said to the lady with the Fancy Feet!! I couldn't believe it. I was so happy and so surprised. He was so wonderful and when I got through my mother was very proud of me. It was a day I will remember for a long time!

Mrs. Jack LaDelle

The Studio

Shortly after that a dance teacher who was a friend of my husbands, approached me and asked if I would help her with three of her little girls. They had entered 3 dance contests and couldn't get beyond 3rd place. At first I started to refuse but then I got to thinking that she was a friend of Jacks and I should help if I could. I told her to bring them over and I would look at their routine and see if I could help.

She brought them to me to see and they were really cute but I decided to throw away their music and routine and start new. I had a lot of fun working with them and creating a number for them that I thought would make them look good. After working with them for several months she entered them into the same contest again and they came in first place.

Later that evening she came to the house and asked if I would continue teaching them that their parents and they were so delighted that they won and she knew she could not put things together like I did. I thought for a few minutes and I did enjoy teaching them and it was a great experience to see the after affects so I told her yes. I did not realize that my husband and she put this together quite a while ago to get me to teach dancing.

Well, to make a long story short, I started off with them and it was shortly after that I met a lady who worked at the hospital and she told me she always wanted to dance. She said she also could probably get some more girls………

I really had no place to teach at that time but I told her I would think about it. Shortly after that I ran into a nice lady who had a dance studio of her own and rented out space. I asked her what she charged and I told her I would like to start with just time for two classes one for my young girls and one for older ladies. Well, that was the start of my dance teaching career in Las Vegas.

I started out just teaching the three little girls and my line of adults, that I called the Whoopie Girls and I had four girls that were called my Naughty Ladies.

My first group of Naughty Ladies with me in the middle

Soon after was my second group of Naughty Ladies!

I was going to find my own studio when my husband found one on Hacienda. I had to put a dance floor in it and I looked for someone to put it in. I found this gentleman and called him and he asked me if I wanted wood or linoleum, when he told me how much wood cost I told him something cheaper. He came to measure my studio and talk to me more about it and his wife came with him. When she walked in she was so excited to see me, she remembered me from the Dunes and she said to her husband I had to have wood because I was a good tap dancer and she reminded him that he had several pieces of wood that were left over from jobs and he could just put them together and make me a floor I could afford since they were all different but just left over from jobs.

He sort of gave her a rough look but he said he would see what he could do. He did a beautiful job of putting together different kinds of wood and I was thrilled, there is nothing like dancing on wood for a tap dancer!

After I got my studio ready I bought over my lines of students and I started advertising. It was great all the people I got. Then the College got hold of me and asked if I would offer my classes for summer to their students. I offered classes in tap, jazz and belly dancing and had great responses. In fact most of my students I have now are from that ad.

It was about that time that I met a nice man by the name of Dick Bingham. He asked if I would be interested to do some shows for him and I said I would love to. He started booking my ladies and me and he became my MC. He had such a good heart and he became a good friend and a good MC. He found all kinds of places to book us and kept us busy for a long time. Unfortunately after about a year or so he passed away. He was so nice and always a good MC, I hated to lose him.

Social Butterflies

The Social Butterflies will be getting together for another wonderfull evening. We will meet on September 28, Thursday night at 7P.M. We will have refreshments and a raffle for prizes.

This will be for only Social Butterflies PAID UP members. Our membership is now closed since we have reached our quota. When you come this month, you will receive a membership card at the door. Our entertainment will be the CREATIVE DANCERS, a variety show directed by DICK BINGHAM and DEE.

We will have a special guest star, FRANKIE RANDALL, who many of you have seen when he did a tribute to a Frank Sinatra Concert outdoors this summer at the Henderson Center. He also sings and plays piano. He has entertained at the Venetian Hotel on the Strip. Frankie's versatality is without limits. He has composed songs and has 2 CD's out. We are thrilled to have him come out to entertain us here in Sun City. Frankie Randal will be accompanied by JOE DARRO. We will also feature BOB SANTIAGO, our Vice President, who will be bringing us music for dancing and your listening pleasure.

Any questions, please feel free to call PEARL at 270-8257.

Not long after that I got a call from a friend of mine up in Sun City and she asked if I would be interested in teaching a class in belly dancing up there in their rec center and I told her yes. We got a great response from that and I started teaching belly dancing up there.

My belly dance class with me in the middle

NORTHWEST VIEW
FEB. 25 EDITION — WEEKLY PUBLICATION ALSO SERVING NORTHWEST LAS VEGAS

Belly dancing adds spice to life

By Scott Gulbransen
View staff writer

For a group of active Sun City Summerlin residents, belly dancing is yet another activity they are learning in the golden years of their lives.

"I had watched a senior citizen woman named DeLois LaDelle perform some belly dancing at a performance here in Sun City and thought it would be wonderful to teach others," said Sophie Cook, an activities director at Sun City. "I thought it was a way we could learn something that was fun and also good exercise."

Cook approached LaDelle and began a dialogue that would end with the performer agreeing to teach a class.

"I was very surprised when Sophie asked me about teaching belly dancing," said LaDelle, who has been a professional dancer and performer for more than 40 years. "The reason it surprised me was older women usually are not interested in this type of dancing."

LaDelle learned the art of belly dancing some 40 years ago when she spent some time in Damascus, Syria. LaDelle said the most common misconception about belly dancing is you have to be young and skinny to perform it.

"I learned the dance from a 60 year-old woman in Syria who was overweight," LaDelle said. "It really is body dancing and it is an expression of who you are and it doesn't matter how old you are or how big or small you may be."

The first class, which met the first week of February, was full and many of the participants were excited at the thought of learning the exotic dance.

"If you would have asked me 10 or even 20 years ago if I would be learning to belly dance I would say no," 62 year-old Muriel Ramsey said. "But I feel comfortable with my body, and it's a way to add some spice to my husband's life as well."

Other members of the belly-dancing class are simply looking for a new way to exercise and keep in shape.

"I'm tired of just walking and playing golf," Regina Lauer said. "This exercises every part of your body and is a fun way to keep my figure."

LaDelle agrees saying belly dancing works the entire body.

"There are so many parts of the body involved and it really is a good exercise activity," LaDelle said. "I don't know that you could have any more fun than belly dancing."

Please see BELLY/4AA

DeLois LaDelle, who has been a professional dancer and performer for more than 40 years, teaches belly dancing classes.

Dance
2AA/Summerlin View/Saturday, August 19, 2000

From 1AA

energetic, and reigning national champions to boot.

The dancers took first place in two 50-and-older categories at the Rainbow Connection's national competition July 24-27 at UNLV's Ham Hall.

Sun City won the ethnic category with its "Magic Woman" routine and the Broadway variety category with "Beautiful Girls," said Cook, who started the dance club in February 1998. She helped organize the Sun City Dance Connection, under which the exotic dancers operate.

"We're excited because this was our first time winning the national competition," she said. "It's more amazing because only seven of the 12 women danced — the others couldn't make it for various reasons."

The women earned the national berth by placing second in the regional competition in Laughlin, Nev. They weren't obsessed with winning a national title, though they'd practiced enough to win, said Gerda Darmstadt.

"We hoped (to win). We hoped hard," she said.

Most of the dancers' year is spent in class — rather than on stage — learning from noted tap dancer DeLois LaDelle.

For many, the group offers camaraderie.

It also offers a chance to rekindle a love for dance, explore a new hobby and get in shape. The dance connection offers 12 dance genres, including ballroom, country-western, jazz, line, round, square and clogging.

Belly dancing is the most popular of the exotic dance offerings, which also include hula, flamenco, Tahitian dance and Filipino folk dance.

"Belly dance is the perfect exercise because every muscle in your body has to be trained," said Darmstadt, who also likes the other exotic dances and is a veteran of folk dancing and ballroom dancing.

"I dance my feet off," proclaimed Gloria Kinpo, who dances in all five disciplines and plans on toe-tapping "until she can't dance anymore."

A hobbyist painter, gardener and tennis player, she took up dance to get back in shape after hip-replacement surgery in 1996.

"It took me about a year to get used to it," she said. "I didn't know if I was going to dance or (be as active as before), but I was sure going to try."

Fellow tennis player Kathleen Hunt lost 1½ inches off her waist in the first four months of the weekly exotic dance class.

"It was hard initially and I ached for a while," said Hunt, who won a silver medal in tennis during the last Senior Olympics. "But once the pain went away, I felt invigorated. Belly dancing is not hard to learn, but it takes patience."

And dedication. As the competition neared, the women practiced two and three times a week and doubled floor time to two hours to hone synchronization, Hunt said. The dance routines last four minutes.

The club decided their competition outfits would carry a Las Vegas showgirl theme — eye-pleasing evening gowns, eye-popping, feather-adorned fans and dainty hats. Soledad Kamzan designed many of the fans, a few hats and her own fire-engine-red gown.

"The (six professional) judges judged a lot on the beauty, design and colors of the costumes," said Kamzan, who was recruited into the club by Cook. "Besides, I like getting dressed up and looking pretty."

The women also like to win, said Cook, who uses dancing to blunt arthritis from knee injuries 10 years ago. Sun City won regional honors last year in the ethnic category.

"We're very happy with our victories," Cook said. "We're also very happy with dancing. It is a great exercise ... it allows us to laugh back at our children."

My husband and I were so surprised at how fast my business was expanding. Then I started entering my students and myself in the Rainbow competition. That was great fun and they all came off with first or second place. I won 1st and was thrilled. I started receiving all kinds of trophies to add to the ones I already had. I have to say all my students made me very proud, they all worked hard and did well.

I kept winning even more trophies and one for the fastest female tap dancer in the nation for 20 years. It was great experience and I truly love to tap.

Anyway, then we started doing shows around town. We did them for the convalescent homes, private parties and as my reputation grew we got many more shows.

Dancer opens studio to pass on knowledge

By Leanne Mieszala
View staff writer

There's no business like show business fo DeLois LaDelle, who is re-living her pa through her students.

After working in the entertainment indu try all her life, LaDelle decided to open he own dance studio, located at Arville and H cienda roads.

Creative Studio, home to De's Dolls, fea tures both group and private lessons in tu dancing and song and dance routines.

To date, LaDelle's clientele includes ? students, ranging in age from 5 to 82.

Ask LaDelle about any one of her student and she's likely to respond as would a prou mother. In fact, portraits of students ado

Please see DANCER/5A

DeLois LaDelle leads a class at her dance studio, located at Arville and Hacienda roads.
Leanne Mieszala/View

Dancer

From 1AA

her walls, and with each photograph comes a story.

"I love my kids," she said. "We have a lot of fun, but we also work very hard."

One of LaDelle's students is 11-year-old Christina De Loera who aspires to be a singer, dancer and actress.

"She teaches me how to sing properly and she also teaches me how to dance correctly and model my movements and how to use the (microphone)," De Loera said. "A lot of things that are part of the entertainment business."

Besides learning a lot, De Loera said the classes are fun.

"She makes it all enjoyable, and if you make a mistake she doesn't yell at us," De Loera said. "She just tells us that we'll get it down if we practice. She's a very good teacher."

In 1995, LaDelle decided to enter herself in a dance contest sponsored by the Rainbow Competition.

After competing against individuals from all over the country, LaDelle was named best female tap dancer in the nation, a title she has gone on to retain the last four years.

"I decided to dance again because my mother had Alzheimer's at that time, and I felt by doing this I might be able to bring back some memories for her," LaDelle said.

After learning of LaDelle's accomplishment, a teacher approached her and asked for assistance in helping three students win a dance competition because they had never finished higher than third place.

LaDelle agreed, and the trio won.

"That's how it all got started," LaDelle said. "All of a sudden, people became aware of my teaching abilities, and before I realized it, I was renting studio space to be able to accommodate all of them."

Finding it hard to always get the studio time she required, LaDelle began making the necessary arrangements to open her own studio.

In addition to her classes at the studio, LaDelle teaches a belly dancing class at the Community College of Southern Nevada and in Sun City. She first became interested in belly dancing after her travels took her to Damascus and Syria.

"Belly dancing is different from what you see in clubs," LaDelle said. "In this form of dance, I instruct my students on how to

Please see DANCER/6AA

Dancer

From 5AA

control their body."

Gloria Kimpo and Penny Juzwinski are two of LaDelle's belly dancing students from Sun City.

"I love it," said Kimpo who has been taking the class for about eight months. "It's something different."

"It's exciting. The crowd shouts and screams all the time," said Juzwinski referring to the group's past performances.

LaDelle said her husband, who recently died of cancer, was her biggest fan and the one who persuaded her to open up the studio.

"He always said, 'You know De, you've done this all your life, and it's something that you've always loved to do and you're good at, so why don't you just teach,'" LaDelle said.

LaDelle considers herself fortunate to have a business that allows her to teach her belove craft.

"I love the entertainmen world," she said. "I still love t sing, and I love to act. It wi always be a part of my life."

LaDelle referred to herself a professional in the past bu doesn't consider herself on anymore.

"I'm just a ham," she said " love the entertainment business and I want to be able to pass th same feeling along to m students."

Those interested in contactin Creative Studio can cal 222-1991.

Creative STUDIO

- Tap
- Jazz
- Belly Dancing
- Stage Presence
- Ballet
- Argentine Tango
- Stage Presentation
- Dance Just For Fun!
- Shows
- Competition
- Swing
- Kundalini Yoga

...and Much, Much More!...

Creative Studio
3400 W. Desert Inn Road • Las Vegas, NV 89102
Telephone/Fax: 702.896.4012
Website: www.creativestudiolv.com • Email: contact@creativestudiolv.com
Designed and powered by 3JM • Las Vegas, Nevada USA

ENTERTAINMENT WILL BE PROVIDED ALL DAY
Brought to you by Bobby Jean Denny, Director of Entertainment for Nevada Senior Olympics. Backgound music provided by Carl Grove.

Bingo
2 for 1 Admission

Double Down Cloggers
Director: Jim Kvool

Sun City Dance Company
Director: Jackie Conville

Westside Academy
Director: Shelby Brown

Dee LaDelle Studio
Director: Dee LaDelle

Nevada Silver Tappers
Director: B.J. Hetrick Irwin

Nevada Senior World NEWSPAPERS

Invites everyone to a day of FUN at the

Lovin' Life EXPO

Henderson, Nevada
Friday, March 16, 2001
at the
Whitney Ranch Community Center
1575 Galleria Street • Henderson

Doors open 9 a.m. - 3 p.m.

It's Free!

- BOOTHS
- EXHIBITS
- ENTERTAINMENT

★ Hourly Drawings $100 CASH
★ Admission
★ Parking
★ Health Checks
★ Product Samples

Free Continental Breakfast!!!
9 a.m.
sponsored by Henderson Seniors Center

CASINOS • CRUISE LINES • FINANCE
RETIREMENT COMMUNITIES • HEALTH & NUTRITION
FOOD • FUN!
(Health screenings available)

FOR MORE INFORMATION CALL JEANNETTE RYDER AT 602-438-1566 EXT. 411

★ Entertainment ★

DeLois LaDelle and Friends
10 am

The Mac Tappers
11 am

The Clogging Desert Stars
12 noon

Silver Belles
1 pm

SUNSET STATION
FREE BINGO AT THE EXPO
SPONSORED BY SUNSET STATION
2 pm

CREATIVE STUDIO PRESENTS

DeLOIS LaDELLE
AND
FRIENDS

A GREAT SUNDAY AFTERNOON SHOW!!

ENTERTAINERS OF ALL AGES

January 9, 2000
2:00 p.m.
2nd floor Ballroom at
Arizonia Charlie's

$7.50 Donation

CREATIVE STUDIO, 3333 Arville at Hacienda

DeLois LaDelle
8602 Redwood Street
Las Vegas, Nevada 89139

• Studio phone: 223-1000 • Home: 906-7160 • FAX: 896-4692

I told my Naughty ladies that I planned to add some of my Whoopie girls to their class so I could have some more Naughty Ladies. One of them was a dance teacher on her own and said she felt like she was much better than any of my Whoopie girls and she would quit if I added them to her class. So I told her that all of them were willing to work and learn and when she said they would never be as good as she was I told her I thought she should give them a chance and again she threatened to quit if I let them join the class, I told her there was the door!. Two of the other girls were friends of hers and she made them quit so I only had one left. I thought it was sad that she felt that way but the Whoopie Girls who joined the class picked up the routines and worked really hard to do them well. I then had some other girls join the Whoopie class and that class grew too.

I also had a little girl start that was 5 years old by the name of Nicole. She was so scared when she started but she loved to tap. She had private lessons and her mother would bring her. She is now 18 and I am so proud of her!

My three older kids were now becoming teenagers and they were doing well.

I had one other young girl and her name was Christina. She was a beautiful young lady and after being with me quite a while she auditioned for Disney and they accepted her. I was so thrilled for her and she is still working at entertaining!

All of a sudden my studio kept growing and growing. In about a year or so after all this happened my new Naughty Ladies entered a contest and one of the other entries was the lady that quit my class. She would not speak to any of the girls or me when she came in. When the results came in my girls won the gold medal and she got 4th place. She left and never even spoke to me.

I was still working for Dr. Kaiser and Dr. Susan Steinberg. I really liked them both and my job but my husband and I talked and he said to me "Honey, you are just overdoing it, your studio is doing so good and I know you love that but you are kind of burning the candle at both ends and I think you need to make a decision about which profession you would like to be in. I have to be honest when I say it was hard for me to make a decision at that point but I knew my husband was right. I had already got my license to teach, I had already paid for my rent of the studio and I knew that it would be hard for me to give up the dancing because that had been the best part of my life.

So I finally went in and gave my resignation to Dr. Kaiser and Dr. Steinberg. Both of them said they were sorry to see me go but wished me luck and told me to keep in touch. I felt sorry at first doing that but as I got back to teaching I realized that that was something I really did love and I was very happy.

We continued doing shows and entering competitions and I was really enjoying my students and I got two new belly dancers that stayed on from the college class. Their names were Halimah and Lea Anne. They also entered the contests and got first place. I was so proud of all my students.

☙ Life Goes On

My life with Jack was continuing to be good. He was still handling conventions and once in a while booked me for some of the shows and even used my girls from time to time. Then one night my little Sinbad, who was now 16 years old almost 17 came out for his nightly cocktail with us.

When he got through he went to Jack and gave him a kiss and then came over to me got upon my lap and I hugged him and he gave me a kiss, then he wanted to get down, I put him down he walked to the door and died. I was devastated. I loved him so much and he had been with me so long. He had been so close to me and lived so long…….I would tease about him being 16 years old and eating chocolate and drinking booze all those years and I had grown to love him so much, I was heartbroken. For months after that every time I would see a Lhasa Apsa I would cry.

Jack bought Foxy to live with us and I was happy for that. He had always been an outside dog but Jack was right when he said that I would very quickly make him an inside dog. Jack knew how much I loved dogs and how lonely I was without Sinbad.

I continued working in my studio and planting things in my yard. We had 2 1/2 acres of land and we fenced a lot of it in sections.

I loved where I lived. Jack had made all of my dreams come true. I was getting write-ups in the paper about my belly dancing classes and about my studio. I felt very grateful and it helped me a lot. I loved my skies, my house, my husband and our dog Foxy and I was very happy at my studio. I thanked the Lord every day for my good luck! I found out that I could just make up dances out of my head and I kept wondering when I would run out of ideas. I guess all of my years in the show business paid off. Most dance teachers I found out went to New York took lessons and got routines and that was the way they taught. Some of them wrote down notes and put them together that way. I don't know how I got the talent to make them up like I did but I had really enjoyed doing that.

The years kept passing and I was very happy with Jack and my studio, Ron came down to see me every so often. I had to put my mom in a home because I found her out by my gate one day and I was afraid she would wonder around the desert. I went to see my mom every other day although she really didn't know who I was. The people were very nice there and the nurses told me I could come see her any time I wanted as long as I understood that I would see a lot of strange things with Alzheimer's patients and that was true. Because I went so often most of the patients thought I was their family because I found out that a lot of people put them there and then would never go to visit. I handled going to see her okay, but I always cried afterwards. There were so many times that my mom was not so kind to me in my life but when she got Alzheimer's I couldn't help from feeling sorry for her and driving home I not only thought about her but all the other people I saw there just waiting to die. There was one time we did a show there while she was there and at the end when I came out she shouted my little girl, I was so surprised but when I stopped and went to her she didn't know who I was……..that was very hard for me, even though I knew that was like that with Alzheimer's.

My brother Bob had been doing well, except for his marriages. He had his first marriage in my back yard in Ohio. It didn't last to long and he divorced her, however about a few months after that they got married again. That marriage didn't last to long and he got a job offer for the space needle in Texas and he moved and went there.

He met another girl there and married her. I felt sorry for him because that marriage didn't work out either. After being married to her for a short time he came back to Ohio while I was working the Public Utilities and I got him a job there. He was working there when I married Jack. He quit the Public Utilities and went to work for a water company in a small town in Ohio and shortly after that he called me and told me he met a girl there and would like to come out to Vegas and marry her in my house.

I liked her very much and was hoping this would be a good match for him. He went back to Ohio and seemed to be happy with her for quite some time.

As time went on I was still happy with my life but I noticed a change in Jack. He would get tired when he walked to long and was getting tired quite frequently. I started to really worry about him but he kept telling me he was just getting older and that is what happens when you get older. One day he got tired walking a short way and I told him he needed to see a doctor, he kept telling me that he was alright then one day he fell and I had to take him to the emergency room. They had a terrible time finding a pulse on him, they put him through all kinds of tests and the doctor told me he had Leukemia. He explained that I would have to bring him in for treatments.

Not knowing much about Leukemia after I took him home I pulled it up on the internet so I could learn more about the disease. I felt so sorry for him. For the next few months I would take him for treatments but I noticed his basic health was failing more every day. His lips got swollen and he lost weight and was just not eating well. I was told to get him some Ensure and he drank that. I was on double run for a year and a half trying to keep up my studio and take care of Jack. He spent a lot of time on the couch in the living room sometimes with me there too. My heart ached for him.

I gathered his information up and sent it to the Mayo Clinic to see if they could do something for him to help him. I sent his information to anyone that I thought might help. I could not believe that I might be losing him. Then one day he started to bleed, it just seemed to come from nowhere. I wanted to call the emergency ambulance but he insisted that I drive him to UMC. I was a nervous wreck and I still don't know how I got him in the car and got him down there. They had a nice man down there at the time that always helped me with Jack and when I pulled up he helped me get him out and put him in a wheel chair, then he parked my car for me while I took him to the emergency room. I found out he was bleeding internally and they worked on him and then put him in a room.

I decided I couldn't leave him and I asked the nurses if they could put a bed in his room, they were so nice to me and I stayed the night. I could not sleep much; I had to check on him. I called everyone and said my studio would be closed and I went home to feed our dog and came back to the hospital. The next few days were terrible and Jack did not want anyone of his friends to see him like he was, when I told them that some of them got mad at me but I had to honor his wishes, I would want him to do that for me if the situation was reversed.

One of the doctors I worked with was very nice and found out what was happening and he came down to see if he could help me. I will never forget his kindness. He went in and talked to the doctors taking care of Jack and he came out and told me that Jack was dying. I told him that wasn't true. I just did not want to believe that I was losing him.

Then a lady from Hospice who had talked to me before came to me and said that Jack was suffering and was holding on because he thought that I would not be all right. I told her he was right, if I lost him I wouldn't be all right. She told me I had to tell him that I would be so he wouldn't suffer any longer. I cried but I finally went in and told him that I loved him and his mother needed to see him and that I would be alright, I gave him a hug and a kiss and I walked out of his room so he couldn't see me cry. Several minutes after that, the nurse came out and told me that he died. I ran back in and tried to wake him up and the nurses came in and held me while I cried. Going home that night was not easy, I felt so lonesome……..

I called Ronnie who was living in California and he told me he had sold his land and was coming to live upstairs in my home to make sure I would be all right. I told him that I would never be all right again. He arrived the next morning. He told me I would have to call the mortuary and make plans for his burial. I looked up the number and called where his mother was buried. They looked up the records and they said that when Jack's mother died (which was before I married him), he had bought coffins for himself, me, my brother Ron and plans to have my mother cremated. He had also left me a note.

When I got there I read it. He said he always loved me and he did not want me to have a funeral for him, he wanted me to have a party with all of my students and friends at my house. I showed it to my brother and I cried more. After we got home I told Ron I couldn't have a party, there was no way I was up for that and Ron said, Sissy you have to carry out Jack's wishes. He just didn't want you to be alone. He has planned everything for you and took care of everything even for me so we have to honor what he wanted. In his way he is trying to make it easier on you because he loved you so much. He did not want you to go through this alone……… I admit it did not sink in that night but through the night I realized all that he had done for me to try to make losing him easier. I appreciated all he did but I still cried through the night.

I got in touch with everyone and told them what had happened and that we were going to have a party at my house that coming weekend because that was what Jack requested. The next morning Ron, Bob and I went to the funeral home and watched while they buried Jack. I was so weak I could hardly stand, I couldn't stop crying……..

The next couple of days were not easy. Ron moved all of his things down here and really took care of me. That weekend we had the party and Ron had taken care of everything except some of the food which I made. As people began arriving I found out that Jack was right, I guess he always knew me so well, it was warming to have my friends and what was left of my family with me. I have to admit I cried a few times but it was wonderful to know that I had friends and family who helped me get through a tough time. The next few months were not easy without Jack but I somehow still felt him in my home. I loved him so much and I finally gave up going threw his things for awhile; I just wasn't strong enough to do that.

About six months after Jack died I lost Foxy. He just died of old age but I was beside myself. I was not doing well when a friend of mine told me I should go down to the animal shelter and adopt a dog. I had never done that before but thought I would give it a try; I was so lonely and needed one so bad. I went down to the shelter and walked through it and I felt so sorry for all of the dogs and at the end of the shelter I saw a white shepherd. He was 2 or 3 years old and we looked at each other and I could tell he needed me as much as I needed him, so I adopted him. He turned out to be every thing I wanted, he would sit next to me in the morning on the couch when I had my coffee and went to the studio with me and watched my girls danced. I really was so happy to have him he even seemed to understand when I had my bad days and would cry because I missed Jack. I named him Spirit because he helped me so much in my lonesome times!

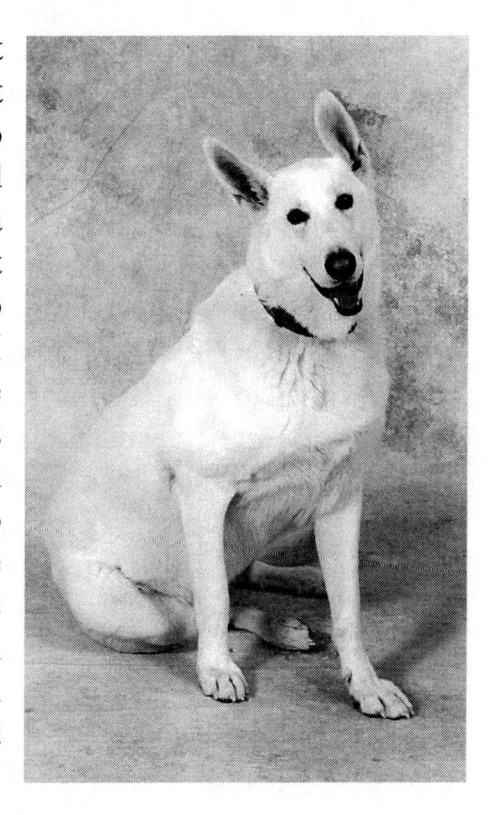

I finally got the nerve to go through Jack's clothes after a year but all of his personal belongings I couldn't touch so I had Ron put them in a box and I told him I would do that later. I tried through the years but I have to admit when I read some of the letters that he had sent me I couldn't really go through all of his stuff until 11 years after he died. But at least at this point I can listen to him sing on his albums and still feel blessed that he was in my life.

I was happy I had my business. I think that Ron and my business were the two things that helped me survive.

Learning to be alone was not easy, even today I still miss him………Even when we were entertainers we could look across a room at each other and feel the love come back. That is something you do not get often in life!

After a couple of years some of my girl friends told me I should get out once in awhile. They took me to a dance at one of the hotels and I was so surprised. Many of the ladies were asking men to dance……in my day that was something you did not do. Anyway I got asked to dance and I did but I wasn't really impressed with any of the men I met. I guess I just wasn't ready to move on. It took me a few years after that before I could go out with any man even though my friends tried to talk me into it! Most of the men I met were looking for a younger woman or a "nurse with a purse" and I really wasn't ready for that. I decided I was just too picky and maybe not ready yet. I dated but found no one that took my breath away.

My studio kept growing and did very well for quite sometime. I did have a problem with the owner that I was renting from. I found out that he was putting other people's electric bills on my bill. He denied it and told me I had to pay those bills or I would have to leave. I spoke to a friend of mine who was very knowledgeable about electric and he checked things out for me and called the utility company and they checked it out and I got all the papers proving what he was doing. He told me to leave if I was not going to pay and I found another studio that I could rent and I left. He took me to court and before we went in they wanted to meet in an office to discuss things, when they did I handed out all of my documentation to his lawyer and his lawyer said never mind, I did not have to pay it and they would pay for my attorneys. I told him that was fine.

Through all of my trials and tribulations at my old studio there was a young man who was a dance teacher who helped me go through some of that drama. His name was Blaine Senior and he was once a dancer in a lot of the hotels in Vegas. He was the one that gave me a place to teach in his studio until I found Creative Studio. While I was renting his studio we became friends and he told me he wanted to learn to sing. I told him he should and I helped him. I really liked his wife and his little boy and I enjoyed renting from him.

I was there for a little while when his mother-in-law wanted to expand and told me she needed the studio I was renting so I started to look for another place. Blaine didn't stay at that studio because he wanted a fancier place; he found one with three studios in it and started renting it. I told him that it was not the studio that bought people in it was the teacher. I tried to convince him but it just didn't work. After a while he lost that studio. He found a smaller one but he had so many dreams. I felt so sorry for him. He had become like a son to me and I couldn't help to feel sorry for him for all the things he went through.

He finally gave up teaching and moved to Utah. He has relatives there and he got a job and is now getting his life straightened out and I am so proud of him. He calls me his adopted mother and that is such a compliment!! He calls me almost every other day and we still stay in contact. I told him he doesn't have to give up his dancing; he can always do that on the side. The difficult thing for a performer is you don't get paid hospitalization and benefits like you do with other jobs. I sometimes look back on that now and think of all that I had with the Public Utilities Commission; I did get to keep my eye and my dental coverage. But I do understand a lot more now than I did, but like I have always said "Life is a learning experience!"

I finally found the studio I am in now and although it was not as big as where I was and I had to put in a floor and make some other changes I was sure it would work and it has.

Creative Studio

FEATURING TAP & ALL FORMS OF DANCE

Come Dance With Us • Open Registration • Visit Any Time

I started doing shows all over Las Vegas from private parties at several of the hotels to retirement centers, hospitals, and anywhere that someone needed a show!! Sometimes we would get $50 for a show and I told the girls that I will always donate anything we make on shows to Alzheimer's or Leukemia. Dividing it between all of us we wouldn't get that much and I would rather give it to a good cause.

My life became nice again even though I still missed Jack. We started doing shows all over town for different organizations, we were at the Paris, the Stratosphere, the Mirage, the Flamingo, the Venetian, .and I became very busy. I found out I really loved to teach and it really didn't make any difference to me whether they had previous experience or not. I always had a saying that if someone wants to do something bad enough and they don't mind working for it they can achieve anything they want! I was also doing a lot of shows for Lynn Burdick in Summerlin, at first I did several things on my own for her then in some of her next productions she asked me to use my girls as well and we all had a great deal of fun in her productions in Sun City!

It was shortly after that I received a call from a man that said he had a stroke and was getting better but always wanted to tap dance. Someone had told him to call me. I told him to come on in. His wife bought him in and after working with him the first time I felt sorry for him because he still could not speak to well and sometimes had some problems but I told him my saying that I believe if you want to do something bad enough and you don't mind working at it you can do anything you want; and he listened. At first it was difficult, but he did really want to do it and he kept trying and he kept getting better.

After teaching him a year he started gradually becoming better and better and stronger. I got tickled that he was doing so well and I thought I would put him in with a line of girls because most men put their shoulders back and like to show off for woman and it worked. He became a big "ham"!! I really liked him and I made him my MC. He was thrilled. He also danced with the Whoopie Girls.

I had so much fun with him. His wife was so nice and we all three went out to dinner and to dance once in awhile. She would dance with him and then I would dance with him. He was a good ballroom dancer and was fun to dance with and I taught him a few new steps he didn't know. I always loved to ballroom dance and did a lot of it when I was a professional entertainer.

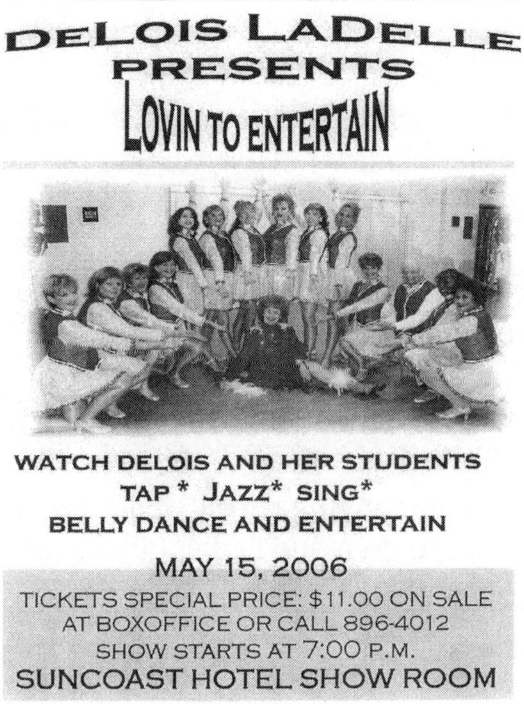

After one of our shows I got a call from a gentleman who said he saw my show and was very impressed with it. He asked me if I would like to do a show at the Suncoast. I told him I would love to do that. I loved it because for me it was like the old days the light men all kidded me and told me they knew that I had been a professional and I really loved doing a show there.

The next day after our first show there I received a call and they booked us back again. I really loved it!

Not long after that Ron met a lady by the name of Annie and moved in with her. I missed him but I was happy he found someone again.

It was also about that time that some of my girls told me about the Ms. Sr. Nevada contest. I told them that was something I didn't want to do because to me that we be boring walking around a stage and waving, I like to get on a stage and dance and sing! Well anyway, I met a friend and she introduced me to the lady who was in charge of it and I became a contestant. I really didn't think I would win but I met a lot of nice people and it was fun.

I did find there were a lot of ladies who were really set on winning. I was surprised at the different things that you had to do: your philosophy of life, your talent, your gown, etc. The night of my competition I was very nervous. I honestly did not think I would win and when they gave me the talent award I was very happy and thought that was it. So when shortly after that they announced me as the winner, I was shocked. I had a lot of fun after that meeting people and attending different places.

Ms. Senior Nevada 2005 2006
Age Of Elegance
DeLois La Delle

A few years after that the lady who had it passed away and the gentleman that had always been with her took over. To this day I am still part of their competitions as one of the previous queens and I get to participate in several different functions over the years.

My Life Like It Is Now

A couple of years after that the economy changed. The college I was teaching for stopped offering my classes because they said most people were taking classes in education because they didn't have the money to spend for fun things. I lost several of my students and even though my Naughty Ladies and my Whoopie group changed ladies they were still all doing my shows and I have always been proud of my groups. My belly dancers Lea Anne and Halimah are still doing great along with my younger lady Nicole!

I lost my dog Spirit. I was really devastated, I had him for about 10 years and he was such a good white shepherd. I knew he was not doing well and I took him to the doctor. He told me he was 13 years old and he thought I really should put him to sleep. I told him I couldn't do that, I cried and asked him if there wasn't something he could do, he said he could give him something and it might help him for a few days. He told me to wait outside and when I went out in the waiting room I started to cry and it dawned on me that I was making him suffer because I couldn't stand to have him die. I have a hard time of letting go of those I love as I found out with my husband, Jack. I asked the doctor to come outside and I told him I was very embarrassed to put my dog through something that would only help him for a couple of days when he felt so bad so I told him to do what he thought best. I cried because Spirit was the first dog I had ever had to "put down"

Shortly after that the Lord took care of me again through an add in the paper that someone was trying to find a home for a shepherd. I called it and the lady said that she had two dogs already but found this one in a vet's office and it had been left without food and water from some people that had just vacated their house and the next door neighbor took it to the vet. When she saw it there she decided to take it home with her but when she got it home he did not like her cats and she was afraid he would kill one so she gave her cats to her mother to keep till she found a home for the dog. I told her I was still so upset about losing my dog I didn't know what to do but if she wanted to bring him over I would take a look at him but I didn't want to promise anything. When she got him here I went outside in my driveway and she opened her truck and he came out and came running to me right away. I looked in his eyes and he was so much like Spirit I couldn't believe it so I told her I would take him and see how it went. She said for me to call her right away if I had a problem and to keep in touch with her, she said she really liked him but she loved her cats too. Well to make a long story short I have him now and I am so happy, he is like my Spirit in so many ways, he sits on the end of the couch every morning next to me while I have my coffee just like Spirit did, almost all of the things he does are just like Spirit. The only difference is that he is a lot younger and much stronger, much like Spirit when he was his age. I have not had the chance to give him the training because of my leg that he needs but he has been so good and so much company I feel very blessed to have him.

Right before Spirit died I started having problems with my left leg. I couldn't understand it because I have been very blessed, never been in a hospital as a patient and never on drugs. When I turned 74 my life changed. They did some tests and found out I have a thyroid problem and when I had my yearly exam for my eyes I found out I had glaucoma and I am now on thyroid pills and drops for my eyes for my glaucoma. I went to a doctor who had been a doctor here for quite some time about my leg. He did an x-ray and said I was just getting older and since I had been dancing since I was three and a half years old my knees were getting old and I had arthritis. He said I didn't need an MRI and that an x-ray shows the same thing. He gave me some shots etc and it helped off and on but my knee became more and more painful. I had to actually lift it and put it in the car it hurt so much. How I got through my shows last Christmas was a miracle!

Finally one of my nurses and some of my students told me my knee was swollen with liquid. They told me to go to another doctor. I spoke to some friends of mine and they suggested I go see Dr. Ong. He was wonderful. He did an MRI and said I had two torn meniscus and my knee was filled with liquid. He said that somewhere in my life I might need a knee replacement but he thought an arthroscopy might give me some relief and help me continue to do some of the things I do for a little longer. I went home that night and talked to Ronnie and asked him what he thought I should do. He said it was really up to me but if I did do it he wanted to be with me. When I told him that I had some friends that would help me he said "Sissy all the things you have done for me in my life, I want to do whatever you need to help you by myself and that is exactly what he did. Well I thought about it and I decided that I was in such pain I should go for it. Dr. Ong sat it up for me. When I had the arthroscopy on my leg Ron drove me to get my surgery done. The nurse even let him come in and talk to me until they were ready for me. The doctor, the anesthesiologist, and the nurse all came in and talked to me before I went in. I told the anesthesiologist that I had never been in a hospital before and never been put under, he said he would be easy on me. I was very scared but I was glad Ron was with me. They let him come in to stay with me till they were ready to perform it. When I woke up Ron was there and said he was going to stay with me that night to help me. They all came out and talked to me afterwards. Dr. Ong told me he cleared out the fluid and mended the Meniscus and that he was going to send me to therapy the next day. Ron took me home with that big cast on my leg and was so good to me. He said he was going to spend the night in case I needed him and that he would take me to therapy the next day. He was so good to me the whole evening, I was embarrassed when it came time for me to get into bed because I couldn't get the stupid leg up on the bed with that cast on it so Ron came in and lifted it up for me. It was even horrible to go to the bathroom. Thankfully I do have things to hold on to in there!!! The next day he took me to therapy and waited for me.

The people in therapy were wonderful to me although I was surprised at the exercises they gave. They were exercises I did when I was eight years old at dance school. I was getting along pretty good although it hurt when they tried to bend it so they let me take the cast off which I hugged them for and go without it. Ron took me home and I really thanked him for all that he did. He said he was going to go to work and would come back by on his way home to check on me. I was surprised after my surgery. Nothing hurt near as bad as it did before the surgery. I have done a show since then and although I know it is not completely healed it is better and I am very happy I had it done. Various changes made me loose some of my older students, so right now I don't really have that many students and basically what I make covers my expenses with a little left over. The Lord always looks out for me and I now I have a Hawaiian group that rents my studio two days a week that has helped a great deal. They are looking for a bigger studio so I know they won't be here long but it is good while they are.

I started going out more often with lady friends and many times we would go into somewhere and there would be some of the old time musicians and they would ask me to get up and sing. Being the "ham" that I am I always did and still do. Sometimes it is just the guys who sing around town that invite me up and that is my fun and joy. I've always loved being an entertainer and that I hope will never leave me. I even rerecorded an old record that I recorded 40 years ago called Daddy was a Preacher and Mama was a Go Go Girl. A rock group recorded it recently called Southern Culture. And now I am writing the story of my life as I have lived it so far. Some parts I've left out but at almost 75 at least I am still teaching and doing shows although I still have to be careful with my leg. I feel very grateful to have done all the things I have done up to this point in my life, I thank the Lord every day for his help and I hope to be able to continue as long as I am physically able. I've always loved to entertain and always felt very blessed to be doing things in my life that I really enjoy. I can't complain if I have to stop someday but for now I am just taking one day at a time and enjoying all the time I have left and to this day I still think I was "Born to Entertain"!

Lovin' to Entertain!
DeLois LaDelle

Addendum
My life in pictures!

These shoes were made for dancing!

123

LOIS PHILLIPS

Let's play dress-up!

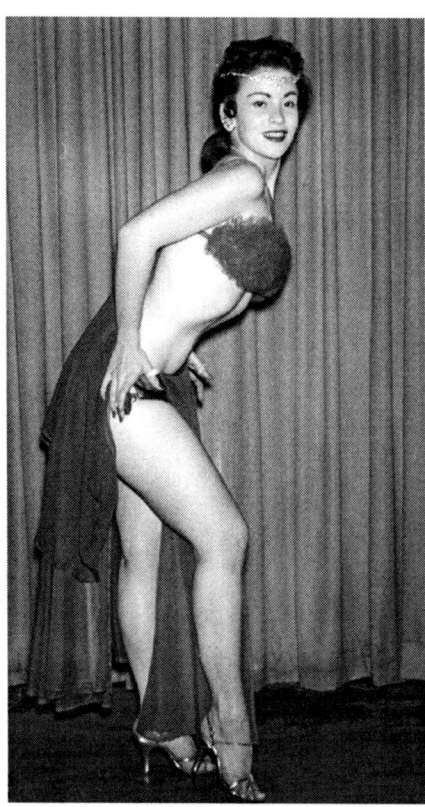

Glamour and gowns!

126

Just for fun!

DeLois Ladelle (Ms. Nevada) sang her heart out

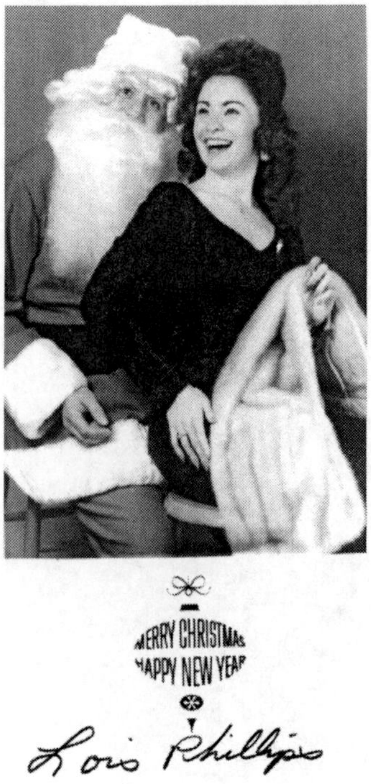
MERRY CHRISTMAS
HAPPY NEW YEAR
Lois Phillips

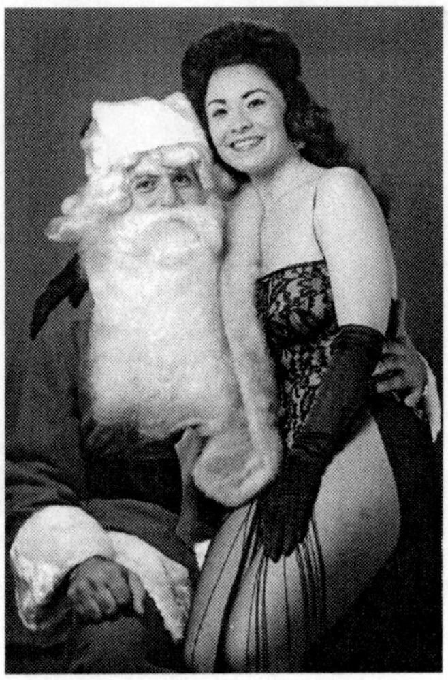

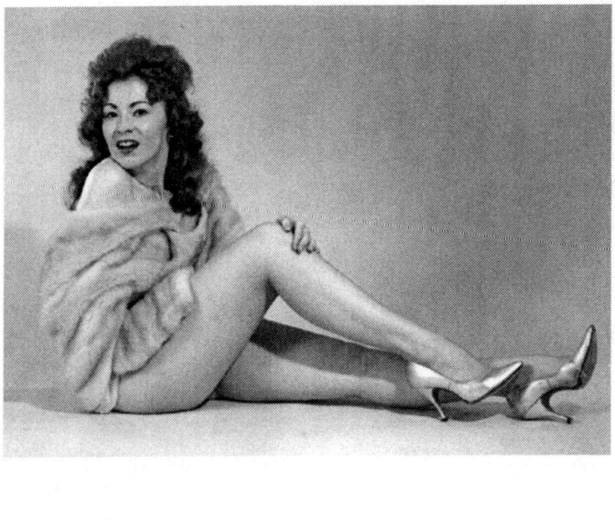

...and she shall have music wherever she goes!

Miss De Lois and her Music Men

Miss De Lois and her Music Men

Miss De Lois and her Music Men

130

Students

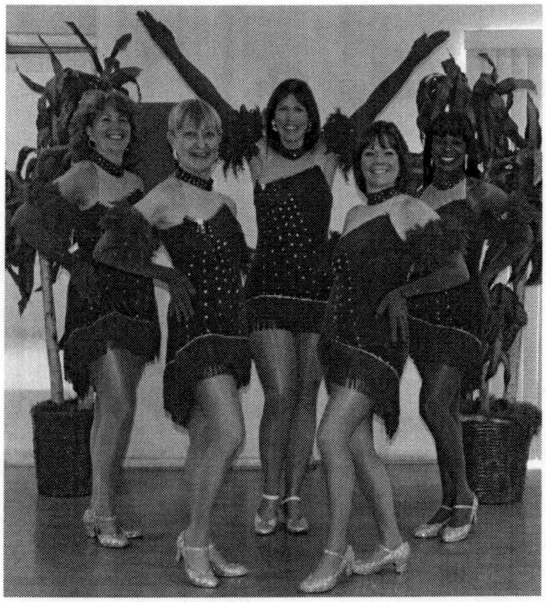

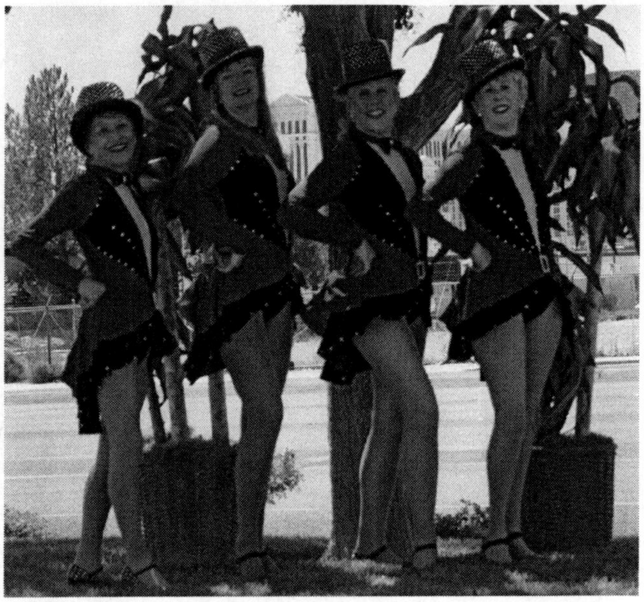